SERVING
A NEW
NATION

The **Institute of Southeast Asian Studies (ISEAS)** was established as an autonomous organization in 1968. It is a regional research centre dedicated to the study of socio-political, security and economic trends and developments in Southeast Asia and its wider geostrategic and economic environment. The Institute's research programmes are the Regional Economic Studies (RES, including ASEAN and APEC), Regional Strategic and Political Studies (RSPS), and Regional Social and Cultural Studies (RSCS).

ISEAS Publishing, an established academic press, has issued more than 2,000 books and journals. It is the largest scholarly publisher of research about Southeast Asia from within the region. ISEAS Publishing works with many other academic and trade publishers and distributors to disseminate important research and analyses from and about Southeast Asia to the rest of the world.

SERVING A NEW NATION

Baey Lian Peck's Singapore Story

Ooi Kee Beng

ISEAS

INSTITUTE OF SOUTHEAST ASIAN STUDIES

First published in Singapore in 2011 by
ISEAS Publishing
Institute of Southeast Asian Studies
30 Heng Mui Keng Terrace
Pasir Panjang
Singapore 119614
E-mail: publish@iseas.edu.sg
Website: <http://bookshop.iseas.edu.sg>

The responsibility for facts and opinions in this publication rests exclusively with the author and his interpretations do not necessarily reflect the views or the policy of the publisher or its supporters.

ISEAS Library Cataloguing-in-Publication Data

Ooi, Kee Beng, 1955–
   Serving a new nation : Baey Lian Peck's Singapore story.
   1. Baey, Lian Peck.
   2. Businessmen—Singapore—Biography.
   3. Singapore—Officials and employees—Biography.
   I. Title.
DS610.73 B13O61   2011

ISBN 978-981-4345-42-2 (hard cover)
ISBN 978-981-4345-43-9 (e-book, PDF)

Cover design by Chris Lim Kah Wai
Cover photos of Dr and Mrs Baey Lian Peck by Ooi Kee Beng

Typeset by Superskill Graphics Pte Ltd
Printed in Singapore by Mainland Press Pte Ltd

CONTENTS

Appendices

FOREWORD

I knew Baey Lian Peck through his work in the Singapore Corporation of Rehabilitative Enterprise (SCORE). I found him public-spirited, willing to give of his time in spite of his business schedule. From SCORE, he went on to other duties for the government. I always found him responsive and diligent in carrying out the duties he voluntarily undertook.

Without people like Baey Lian Peck, Singapore could not have been as well run. We have decentralised many of the functions of government into institutions run primarily by public-spirited men and women. The government supplies the secretarial staff. Baey Lian Peck was one such man.

Lee Kuan Yew
13 June 2011

ACKNOWLEDGEMENT

It is not given many to have the opportunity to listen to a major actor of a period just passed telling his or her life story in detail and explaining the recent flow of events that one knows about only in passing as reported news. I had that chance, and when interviewing Dr Baey Lian Peck about his experiences and achievements, the contingency of life became evident and the immediacy of the individual's role in events became shockingly apparent.

This is a blessing not to be taken lightly. Working on this book has meant that I got to know Dr Baey well. I will not say "very well", because he is a surprising multifaceted man whose work in governmental bodies influenced Singapore's development greatly, and whose business activities spanned the world in an unobtrusive and unknown way. The breadth of this man's activities is simply amazing, even now in his old age.

It has been easy writing this volume because Dr Baey is always inspiring and always willing to share of himself. I thank him and his wife, Daisy, for their warm patience during our interviews.

I am also most grateful to Ambassador K. Kesavapany and Mr Tan Keng Jin for bringing this project my way, and for the confidence they had in me that the book would be done in time for Dr Baey's 80th birthday on 13 July 2011.

Ooi Kee Beng
10 June 2011

INTRODUCTION

When the suggestion to write a book on Dr Baey Lian Peck was put to me by ISEAS Director K. Kesavapany in mid-2010, I must confess that I felt very doubtful. I had just put in three years of work on a book on Dr Goh Keng Swee, and was looking forward to getting back to studying Malaysian personalities from the *Merdeka* years. Not another Singaporean, I thought.

But I had no idea who this Dr Baey was. In fact I had never heard of him, and none of my peers had heard of him. This was not strange, since I began living in Singapore only in 2004. And so, to be fair to the Director, I said I would have to meet the man first before I decided. The head of ISEAS' Public Affairs Unit, Mr Tan Keng Jin, arranged for the three of us to meet for lunch at the Singapore Cricket Club.

It turned out to be a very entertaining meal. Dr Baey was obviously a charismatic individual. Most significantly for me, he was clearly a very frank and honest person, and he had a lot of stories to tell. I was hooked. I had to find out more about him and his improbable tales.

I now think that it was exactly because I had just finished a book on a Singaporean leader that I felt drawn towards the story of Dr Baey Lian Peck. What is always not sufficiently present when authoring a biographical account of great leaders like Dr Goh are the soft voices and untold tales that lurk in the shadows, without which that main plot would not be plausible. In fact, the main plot is fatally bland unless one assumes the existence of these sub-plots.

And yet, the supporting cast in the big drama of nationhood is seldom studied seriously. This is a failing on the part of historians. These sub-plots are stories in their own right.

In that important sense then, the project I was being offered promised to still a disquiet that had settled upon me following my choice to base my book on Dr Goh largely on his writings. The adjoining and the underlying stories began to seek my attention.

Now, Dr Baey does not have a soft voice, but his stories definitely do need telling. As I was to find out, his contribution to Singapore's success was greatest in the country's early decades. That is why his name is unknown to the young.

A book must develop organically, and one must let the subject seek out its best presentation. This became evident to me when I began putting pen to paper [fingers to keyboard, actually]. My training as an academician got in my way immediately, and whatever formal style I chose to use seemed to empty the text of what I knew had to be its essential emotive content.

Telling Dr Baey's story without conveying his enthusiasm, his commitment and his warmth would be a literary crime. And so, in the end, it became obvious. I had to settle for a First Person Narrative. Dr Baey's story must be told in his own words. I must take on the role of the amateur weaver of a rough tapestry, and the multi-coloured wool must come from him.

This book is thus based on many interviews that I had with him between July 2010 and February 2011 at his apartment at The Caribbean in southern Singapore. Other major sources that I used include his meticulously collected private papers, as well as the transcription of oral history interviews he had given to

Mr Santanu Gupta between September and November of 2008 for the National Archives of Singapore.

Dr Baey is a man fascinated by how he came to play such an important role in the life of so many people who were in dire need. He credits his father for teaching him all the important things he knows, but unlike his father, he became much more than just an enviably successful businessman. He became a public servant, and it is at that nexus between being entrepreneurial and public-spirited that so much of his ingenious innovations came into being.

Just when he was succeeding as a businessman, Singapore became an independent but anxious country. This placed him in a potentially influential position. And once he came to the attention of Singapore's first generation of leaders such as Dr Toh Chin Chye, Mr Lim Kim San, Mr Chua Sian Chin, Dr Goh Keng Swee and Mr Lee Kuan Yew, he became a useful personality they could recruit whenever a social crisis threatened.

Each time, Dr Baey answered the call and each time, he rose to the challenge. Born the son of a born businessman, he developed a sixth sense for solving problems, be these social, economic or — in later years — spiritual.

And he did it all for free.

As he likes to note, all in all, over the years, he spent sixty years being chairman of statutory boards, and a hundred years being a board member. This is not technically correct. Many of the boards he was involved in were not statutory boards, such as NTUC Welcome or Ngee Ann Technical College or the Engineering Industries Development Agency (EIDA). But they do add to the overall impression that his contributions to his country were profound and numerous. What's more, his work on a major statutory board, i.e. the Housing & Development Board, is not even discussed in this book.

His is definitely a Singapore story, and one that Singaporeans should know about and take pride in. While his life reflects the suffering, the uncertainty and the enthusiasm of his people over the last eighty years, it is his role in building the country he loves so dearly that provides both exciting insights into the problems that a new nation must face and much needed reminders of the choices a new citizen of a new nation must make.

Chapter 1

BORN A BUSINESSMAN

MY CHILDHOOD

My father Baey Kim Swee had three wives. That was not strange in those days. Many men had many more. My grandfather also had three, incidentally.

Now, my father separated from my mother, who had two sons and four daughters by him. I wanted to be different on that score, and when I married many years later, I wrote a letter to myself when my wife was pregnant with our first child, to be opened twenty years later. And in that, I promised myself that I would not have more than one spouse (see Appendix I).

When I opened it before the family twenty years later, I had of course forgotten its contents. My daughter took strong objection to a paragraph: "If you have to womanise, pay for it".

On reading the letter, I saw that I had accomplished much more than I had set out to do. To be sure, Singapore as a whole had developed during that time beyond what anyone could have dreamt of. Such were the times. I then typed another letter — eight-pages long — to myself, to be opened ten years hence. That, I am afraid, I should not publish. There are people who would take offence at the things mentioned therein.

My grandfather — a Hokkien — was the one who came from China. He was a rice merchant, and I remember him being served opium, which was a drug for the upper classes. He died when I was three or four years old, and I remember him only vaguely.

My father was born in Singapore, and unlike his siblings, studied English. According to him, kids in those days could only study for six years locally. After that, they had to go off to England if they wished to do more studying. Before the war, he had a shop in Kallang Road. That was where I was born, on 13 July 1931.

He also started a petrol kiosk in Crawford Street that year. He knew Lee Kuan Yew's father, who also worked for the Shell Company.

Later on, he acquired two shop houses on Kallang Road, No. 77 and 79, and did very well, thanks to the good location. Hardware was his business — nuts and bolts and screws and all sorts of things that you might require in the home and in construction.

I still remember one of my grandmothers, his third wife. She was a very religious person. I can still imagine her doing her chants in the back room, early in the morning, around 4 am.

I slept under the table in those days, and had a box there as my cupboard where I put all the little things I owned. The house was not small and there were many of us. Her chanting went on every morning, and in the end, I knew all those chants by heart without understanding them. Today, I am a devout Buddhist, and I think that is partly because of her.

I began attending school when I was about eight and my father would give me $1.50 a month — 5 cents per day — that included buying my own lunch. I had to keep account of how I spent that sum. I soon learned how to do it wisely. I was also given 25 cents in the weekend for the movies. That was what the cheapest cinema ticket cost then.

My father went to the Anglo-Chinese Free School in Amoy Street until Primary Six. He was a very independent man. My own education was interrupted by the Japanese invasion. I had done three years of schooling by 1942, and had to finish the rest after the Second World War in accelerated classes and completed the final three standards of my secondary education within one and a half years. I was eighteen by the time I was done. That was all the basic schooling I ever had.

Throughout my life, I remained an avid reader of books though. I managed to get a Diploma in Business Management from London through a correspondence course. But this was after I was married, and it took an awfully long time to complete.

My father was not in the best of health in his later years. Hard living took its toll. Our family doctor was Dr Ong Swee Law. He later became the chairman of the Public Utilities Board. One day, he told my father that if he followed his instructions, he could live another ten years. But if he continued with his bad food habits of eating suckling pigs and Peking Duck and his smoking, he would not last more than six months.

My old man came home that day and told all of us that he was going to die within six months. He was going to continue living the way he had done and refused to exist like "a prisoner". He was a regular at all the top restaurants, going to each for their special dish, whichever that may have been. Other dishes were ordered just as accompaniment.

Dr Ong sent my father to Mount Alvernia after he suffered his second heart attack. He was put in the VIP section, watched by a nurse on 24-hour duty. Now, he would sit there and watch

TV with his eyes closed, and with the volume screwed up to the maximum. He was half-deaf.

Understandably, the man next door was irritated by this, and complained. The superintendent came and saw my old man sitting there with his eyes closed as if asleep, but with the TV on and the sound at full volume. Needless to say, the nurse got a scolding for leaving the TV on despite her protest that the patient was actually awake. Each time the nurse switched the TV off the patient immediately shouted: "Don't you touch my TV!" The nurse was crying when I next came to see my father, and asked that I explained things to the superintendent before she ended up getting the sack. So I had to do that.

As I said, my father was a very independent man, an eccentric guy who didn't care too much about rules.

He soon found staying at the home deadly boring, and so asked the nurse to take him around the corridor in a wheelchair. He then wished to take the elevator down to the ground floor. The sly old man had arranged for his driver to be waiting there. At the entrance to the home, he demanded that the nurse follow him into the car. Amidst protests, she got in and off they went to his restaurant for his favourite dishes, which would have included dishes like suckling pig, shark's fin and bird's nest soup.

That was his style. On his last day, he took the car to his office, had a look around, went home, went to the toilet, and died, quite painlessly. He was in his early seventies.

My mother was his first wife, but she found it impossible to live with him, and so divorced him and left with my elder brother. I stayed behind, along with my two sisters, who from then on acted as mothers to me. It was they who taught me to be independent. There were two younger sisters who were given away. One of them did quite well later in life.

My father loved to hunt flying foxes and would distribute his kill among relatives and friends. He became good friends with a farmer that he met on these trips, and gave one of the younger girls as the betrothed to this man's son, who was a leper. Later in life, we discovered that this sister was doing badly. I remember my elder sisters demanding of my father that she be brought back into the family.

This he did, and she was given a house where she lived until she died about ten years ago.

My mother and brother had moved out, as I said earlier, and lived on Balestier Road. I remember my mother coming to visit me at school, which was the only place she could get to see me, bringing me an apple now and then. My father had forbidden her coming to the house. I would slip away sometimes to visit her as well. She passed away of consumption when I was about eight years old.

I had my first business venture when I was about ten. I got one of my father's employees to buy me cartons of cigarettes. They came in packets of ten. I would then open the lid of the boxes up and display the individual cigarettes on a condensed milk case. I displayed them by the counter at a nearby coffee shop, and sold them one at a time. There were perhaps three brands being sold altogether.

I was making money, at least until someone ratted on me to my father. Needless to say, I got a whacking and my goods were all confiscated. I was supposed to be studying, you see.

THE JAPANESE OCCUPATION

My brother would come by to see me as well, and once gave me a bicycle as a present. But he died, also of tuberculosis, several years later during the Japanese occupation. I remember he would place me on the handlebars of his bicycle and we would cruise along the roads. It was he who taught me how to handle the Japanese guards who were stationed at specific points along road junctions. One must disembark, bow to the guard, push the bicycle along for a bit, and then get back on. Otherwise, you risked a whack on the head from the guard.

According to my brother, when the Japanese soldiers reached Singapore, someone had put up a Kuomintang flag along Bukit Timah Road, instead of the Union Jack. When the advancing Japanese saw that, they retreated across the Causeway, due to whatever fearful experiences they might have had in the fighting in China. But the next day, they returned and slaughtered any Chinese they could find in the Bukit Timah area and beyond.

That was what my brother told me.

He once told me that he and two or three other guys had been out bicycling, and were stopped by a soldier and were charged for something or other. They knew they would probably be killed, and so in desperation they managed to kill the soldier instead, and escaped. That was what he told me. But at that time, I didn't believe him. I mean, how do you kill a Japanese soldier?

I remember he once told me there was something I had to see along Collyer Quay. So we cycled there. Three amputated heads were hanging in the hot sun from lamp posts on public display, covered with buzzing flies. They must have been there for a week. They were supposedly Indonesians who had been caught in some act of robbery. So, their heads were chopped off.

There was an occasion early in the occupation, when we were all ordered to gather in a field in Kampung Kembangan for identification purposes. There were two queues leading to two tables placed in the open. A torn cloth was tied to our left wrist and a mark was chopped on it. You were not allowed to take it off; that was your identity, supposedly. But of course, it was all a facade. What they wanted to do was make some arrests. Those wearing spectacles and those who were strong and able-bodied were taken away. They never came back. They were shot, although we didn't know it at the time. I was only twelve, too young to be killed.

I remember the women present would have their heads shaved to minimise the risk of being raped. Once we saw a girl being chased by two Japanese soldiers. She was screaming in fright and ran into a Chinese temple. I heard later that her body was found in there, she had been raped. This was in the earlier period.

Once, Japanese soldiers came into a coffee shop and ordered everyone to stand up. I was very young so I was allowed to move away. The rest were ordered to line up and hold up their left hand. The officer walked down the row of men with a Taiwanese man next to him carrying a big cloth sieve, similar to the kind you use to make coffee. The soldier took off watches from those standing there and dropped them into the sieve. After he had reached the fourth or fifth person, someone further along the queue took off his watch and hid it in his pocket.

The soldier did not show any change in expression, but when he got to that man, he suddenly drew his sword and chopped his hand off and dropped it into the sieve. This got everyone else further down the line to quickly put their watches back on. I saw blood shoot out into the air. That was one of the scariest moments of my life.

Incidentally, I should also mention that among the first group of soldiers to overrun Singapore were many Koreans. They were the rough ones. Korea had by then been a Japanese colony for quite a while, as you would know. The Japanese placed these troops in front to do the initial fighting and dying for them.

The soldiers would walk around at night looking for women, and as a precaution, my father put up vertical iron bars in all the windows in our house. That wouldn't really have stopped them, so he actually had a secret room made. This was not an attic or anything like that. That would have been what the soldiers would have looked for immediately. We had a hidden room instead, and all the women, including myself, would hide in it whenever we heard their boots approaching. I would be scared stiff, breathing very loudly in fear, and even peeing on myself. I was just a child then.

Fearing for my life, and hearing the rumour that the Japanese were in the habit of taking young boys away to Japan to be raised as Japanese to fight for their motherland, my family made the effort of darkening my skin and putting me up with the family of our Malay gardener who lived in an attap hut within the very large compound of our home.

So, for almost a year, I stayed with them and learned a lot. I learned how to make Malay *kueh*, and his son, Ali, and I, would walk along the streets with some goats, calling out our wares for sale. I even learned to eat live grasshoppers. You pull off the head and the legs; flatten the body with your palms and then pop the thing into your mouth. I never learned what the flattening bit was for.

Now, my father was an innovative man. He actually did some tinkering with an old Fiat so that it actually ran on steam from charcoal, believe it or not. He also had uncanny foresight. When he heard that the Japanese were in Burma, he knew it was a matter of time before they were in Singapore. He was certain that the British would not be able to withstand their advance.

So what did he do? He closed down his import-export business and went and bought himself a $42^1/_2$-acre dairy farm out in the countryside, along Tampines Road. I moved there after a while, and that was basically where I spent the rest of the occupation.

I, a twelve-year-old lad, was put in charge of the dairy farm, and the farming as well. We grew long beans, watermelon and such like, and we reared pigs, goats, ducks, chickens and cows. There was a bull, I remember, who would be fed as many as fifty eggs at a time after mating.

Our pigsty had a floor sloping into a pool. This made it easy to keep the sty clean and the pig waste was simply washed into the pool every morning. This pool overflowed into a second pool, where the waste would remain. This second pool would in turn overflow into an enormous third pool where we grew water hyacinths and kept fishes. The water hyacinth was harvested daily to feed the pigs. So my old man had this recycling system going already back then.

Incidentally, it was in the hyacinth pool that I learned to swim.

After some time, signs appeared on the coconut trees along the road, notifying us that we were under the jurisdiction of the 2944 Butai (Military Force). One day, two trucks of soldiers arrived. Luckily, my father could speak Japanese and an arrangement was made with them. Every other week, trucks would arrive to carry off half our produce. What was surprising was, they would then provide us with things we did not have, such as textiles, sugar, salt and rice. So, given the fact that my father had also bought eighteen kelongs out in Bedok, the family was very well supplied during this time.

We still had our warehouse in town, full of hardware and bolts and nuts. These were taken away by the Japanese. Our loyal watchman, however, insisted that the officer in charge left him a note to say that the army was taking these items. This, he said, was to prove to his boss that he had not taken them himself. The officer understood and left a note.

My father then used that note to accompany an invoice that he sent to the Japanese administration. Believe it or not, he was given a compensation of $1.5 million in Singapore dollar notes.

You may be wondering how it came about that my father could speak Japanese. Well, my grandfather had a provision shop at 42 Prinsep Street. I remember him owning a trishaw that boasted two impressive brass lamps on each side which were always being polished. That was the grand motorcar of the day. His clients were largely Indians living in the area. My father worked for him.

Nearby was a ten-cent store run by a Japanese man called Jo Dai. My father used to hang around the store and Jo Dai would teach him Japanese. He picked up enough to get along, and the two became quite close as friends.

Now, before the Japanese occupied Singapore, there were many donation drives carried out in the colony to help fight the Japanese in China. This was just after Manchuria was invaded in 1931. Most people would contribute as a matter of form; my father as well. This was all recorded, however. After the Japanese came, these records fell into their hands. So the Kempeitai arrested him and tortured him for 18 whole days. This was at the YMCA building.

What saved him was this. One day, while he was being interrogated in his cell, he saw someone in uniform walking by who looked like Jo Dai. He called out to him and he came over: "Hey, what are you doing here?" My father told him his story, and Jo Dai saw to it that he was immediately released. My father soon came to realise that Jo Dai had all this time been a spy for the Japanese military. He was a civilian general.

Thanks to this new connection, my father was able to get quite a few of our friends released.

I remember going to the kelongs to fish for sharks. We would have a series of baited lines with glass balls as floats attached to a kerosene can, placed on a shelf, with the end of the rope tied to a sampan. The fall of the can would make quite a din when you got a catch. A shark can pull your boat along for a quite a while, until it runs out of steam. You then draw it back to the boat. Now, one thing we learned from the Malays was that a shark becomes very docile once you pour fresh water into its mouth. It actually stops struggling then.

Once, two relatives and I went on a sampan rowed by a Malay man out to one of these kelongs. Before reaching it, someone stood up, capsizing the boat. Luckily, the boat man was wearing a huge overcoat which kept him afloat, and everyone hung on to him. I surprised everyone by being able to swim, and I swam to the kelong. You see, without my father knowing, I had learned to swim in our dirty ponds. That now saved my life.

All in all, we did very well during the occupation. We were producing more than we had the delivery network to handle. We had a lot of leftover fish every morning despite the daily auctioning. Little sharks and unwanted fish would be taken home. We had more than what our relatives and friends could consume, so we would distribute the rest to the villagers, our neighbours, along with textiles, salt, eggs, and whatever.

I thought this was a forgotten matter until some years ago, when my second son, Charles, was getting married. A friend of one of the relatives of the bride recognized the unusual name of Baey on the invitation card and wondered if I was related to Baey Kim Swee. After I told her I was the son, she said that her family was one of those who received those gifts, and was actually saved from starvation by them.

That statement touched me deeply.

Back in those days, there was only one family with the surname Baey. My father wanted to differentiate himself as much as possible from newcomer Chinese. He was a Baba, you see.

So he took a deed poll and spelled his name B-A-E-Y. Today, you do have a lot of Baeys who are not related to us.

Later in the occupation, we would see lines of emasculated and skinny prisoners of war being marched pass our farm. We didn't know then that these were mainly Australians. They would walk from Changi Prison along Tampines Road, to whatever place I never quite worked out.

But after a while, through signs and a word dropped here and there, we learned that these prisoners were desperately in need of salt. You see, they were suffering from beri-beri, the deficiency disease. What the adults told us to do was to throw little packets of salt at them, as if we were throwing stones. After a while, the prisoners realized that salt was being chucked at them, and so would pick them up.

The Japanese never caught on.

Now my father's uncanny foresight was right on the money again when the Japanese left. He was sure that the Japanese notes — banana notes, as they were called — would very quickly become worthless, and so told us to use them all up; every single note. So we actually had none of that money when they were finally declared worthless.

Apparently, my old man was old enough to remember what happened to the German economy in 1918, when the deutsche mark became useless after the Kaiser was defeated. He was sure the same thing would happen in the Japanese territories. He was right.

There was a friend who did not agree with him and went around buying up those notes on the cheap. Needless to say, he was shattered when the war ended.

Once the British were back, my father sold off the kelongs but kept the farmland. This was acquisitioned by the Singapore Housing & Development Board some years later.

Now, as a further sign of his farsightedness, he managed to import all sorts of things just when the war ended. In fact, half the contents in the first cargo ship that docked in Singapore during the British Military Administration (BMA) were imported by my father. He had been placing orders for cement, asbestos sheets and other building materials. These were kept by the BMA authorities on arrival and could only be release against confirmed purchase orders.

Aside from building materials, my father also foresaw the need for food following the end of the war. So, he imported these from Australia: asparagus, tomatoes, corned beef and juices, as well as plum pudding and other canned foods. But what he did not count on was the British military auctioning off its own excessive store of canned stuff. So prices dropped sharply, and among the products my father imported then, the least sellable was plum pudding. My family ended up sustaining ourselves on plum pudding for ages. Until today, my sisters still use the phrase: "Don't play plum pudding with me" to mean "Don't fool around with me".

MEETING THE WIFE

I went back to the Anglo-Chinese School, as did my future brother-in-law. He was a member of a badminton club near his home on Grange Road. I would join in. There were always many young girls attending as well. But it was his sister who caught my eye. She was only fifteen at that time — Daisy Tan Poh Hiang, the cutest thing around. She was so sweet and young that everyone called her "darling" in those days.

They are a Teochew family.

One of the things I learned from my father was to go around with a tin of cigarettes which one could offer potential clients.

And then while smoking together, one could talk business. So that was my trademark, a pocket bulging with a tin of cigarettes. Daisy used to laugh at me for it.

I was attracted to her, as you will have gathered by now. It turned out that I had luck on my side. I seemed to have the support of her mother, Ang Cheng Im, who seemed to favour me and was very kind to me. I was very touched. After all, I grew up without a mother.

Later on, with my father doing well in business, I was the only young man who went round in a car. One day, I think I was twenty-one then, her aunties took me aside. Since I was close to her and I kept calling her darling, they wanted to know what my intentions were. Well, they were honourable, of course. My father had been wanting me to get married since I was seventeen or thereabouts. But I was not really interested in women until I was about twenty. When asked out by girls to the movies, I would enquire if they were paying for me or not. I was a real cheapskate back then. In the early days, the only present Daisy got from me was a pencil box.

I was very possessive as well. I would take her to school and bring her back in my car. This was after she told me how men would push towards her on the buses. One day she fell down from that kind of pushing, so I decided that I would drive her from then on.

Now, my father loved to dance. He would hold dance parties at his place on Sims Avenue. Happy World was also a favourite joint for him. Well, while we were at one of these parties, the manager of the Mercantile Bank, an Englishman, was showing great interest in Daisy, and kept dancing with her. That was when I decided it was perhaps time we got married. So I told my father there and then.

His advice was that I should marry the Chinese way. I didn't quite understand why that was important, and said I was planning to get married in the civil court. He replied: "Don't be stupid. If you do that, don't you know that you will not be allowed to marry another later on? You will live to regret it."

I said: "No, no. I am not going to have a second wife. I am marrying only once." I was right. Daisy and I happily celebrated our fiftieth golden wedding anniversary at the Ritz Carlton on 27 May 2006 with 600 guests attending (see Appendix VII). A Chinese marriage meant that you went through certain rituals, like the tea ceremony. It was recognized by the authorities as a customary marriage. Under British law, however, you were still not married. Anyway, we got married on 27 May 1956 at the civil court.

After I was married, I worked for my father for $67 a month. In the old Chinese way, my father would pick up all the bills but his word was law. He had two wives living in the same bungalow. Daisy worked as a secretary for him. He was a frugal man and would use the back of calendar pages for notes. I would then type these out for him. When Daisy came into the picture, she took over that job.

We had a room in my sister's house, which was adjacent to my father's. Even after the four kids had come, all six of us lived in that one room, the kids on double-decker bunk beds. Barbara is the oldest. She is one year older than Henry who in turn is one year older than Debra. Charles is the baby in the family, three years younger than Debra. All our children studied overseas — in America and in Japan, one graduating in Economics, one in Commerce, the third in Mathematics and the fourth in Arts. They are all back here in Singapore now, married with kids.

FAMILY MEALS

Most of what I know I learned from my old man. This includes certain habits. He would write notes on the back of old calendar sheets and on used envelopes. That was what people used to do.

One tradition that my father created was the family lunch every Friday. We always tried to have a get-together once a week. This tradition has been continued, and my kids and the grandchildren drop by every Saturday for a family dinner. Daisy is the cook and after all these years, she has become an adept. When they can't make it, they will call. It is now an obligation, a custom. I must say this has been a very important thing that has kept our family very close. The grandchildren are especially close to each other, meeting and being together so often, be they Baeys or Tans or Thiangs. I hope they can carry on the family meal tradition. I suspect they will. Already now, they all look forward to it every week.

What I want to tell the young is, when an opportunity comes, you must be able to see it, and you must go into it wholeheartedly. Recognizing the opportunity is of course the key. You could say I had the gift, but I think it is more accurate to say that it was due to early training. My father taught me things at our family dinners through his stories; and that is what I have in turn been doing with my family, having regular dinners with them and learning from each other.

I have been in business for over sixty years, so the things I will talk about are just the tip of the iceberg. Some things that I learned from my father were very important. I have had much use of that knowledge, and I am at a point in my life when I wish to pass it on. So, if my story can excite just a couple of young people to do good and to be productive, then it would have been worth it.

Any project one gets into must be seen as a living thing. One must see long term and one must look as broadly as possible. And when you do things well, you see that other things start coming to you without you looking for them. If you are competent in what you do, then it would be silly of others not to try to make use of you, wouldn't it?

I was born right in the middle of the Great Depression, and my father was always a tough taskmaster. As a child, I listened to him and other grown-ups go on endlessly about jobs and unemployment. So, I thought in terms of business and getting along already at an early age. After a while, it becomes a matter of habit. My children can do very well in business, no matter what their present occupation is. They were also imbued with a certain way of thinking when young. As a result, most of them went into business. One of my grandchildren wants to be a doctor, which makes me very happy. We need something other than business people in this family.

Another man who was very important to me was Henry Augusta Forrer, an English magistrate. This was after the Second World War. I had joined the Swing Badminton Party and he was the patron. That was how I got to know him. He was like a father to me. He taught me all sorts of things, including German, etiquette and civic responsibility; things like that. These were things a businessman like my father would not have taught me.

I wanted to get a motorboat, but needed a place to put it. Now, Forrer had access to a beach. He allowed me to put my five-horsepower boat there on one condition, and that was that I had to cart away the rubbish he would collect on the beach, and dump it for him deep in the sea. I soon found out that he would walk along the beach to collect any rubbish he could find, broken glass, rusty tin cans and others and this was what I then carried away to dump. His maid kept a rooster that would crow at the break of dawn. In order not to disturb his neighbours, each night, he would have it kept in a basket with the lid on. You see, the rooster could not crow without stretching its neck!

He had a great sense of social responsibility, that man. That was why I named my first boy Henry, after him. One cannot just have benefits. Benefits come with responsibility. Forrer died in

1969, when I was away in Indonesia. I was not around when he passed away.

Good habits can be cultivated, that is my point. The Americans have something called the Shadow System. What you do is have someone always follow you around while you do things. That is how that person will learn. In my case, I observe a situation and immediately see what the needs are. Supplying that special need became my way of doing business. Of course, you have to do your homework. You see the need, you do your calculations, you study the practicalities, and you decide if it is worth investing in. Not all ideas will bear fruit. Ideas have to be developed upon. Over time, and as you have more capital, this developing of ideas becomes easier or more realisable.

INTO THE FAMILY BUSINESS

After the war, I helped my father in his business. Those were bad times. Our home had no paved roads; no piped water either. What we had was a well on the grounds. This was in Kampung Kembangan. There was also a tap by the road where one could fetch more water if needed. He had a car, but we had to get to school by bus. He wouldn't drive us, saying that we needed to know our own way around.

The Anglo-Chinese School had implemented accelerated promotion. We were taught at double the normal speed, and naturally the subjects were more limited. We had English, Arithmetic and three or four other subjects. After I reached the same level of schooling as my father had, he insisted that I left school: "If I can manage with that level, so can you." That was his logic. I was then in standard six. The classification had changed, instead of primary one to six, it became primary one and two followed by standard one to nine. I had studied up to standard one before the war and was later placed in standard four. I protested, saying that we could now move higher without leaving the country. That didn't help. But he was right. We were studying a lot of English grammar in school. I can truly say that I learned tremendously from him. All the important and useful things that I knew, I learned from him, not from school and not from books. He told me that with Chinese businessmen, if you followed whatever was in the books, you would never get anywhere, except perhaps with the British.

And so, I left to join him in his hardware business. This was in 1948. His second wife had a son and a daughter, while the third had two boys and a girl. All of us lived in the same house. This was all very traditional, and was despite his English education. And all of us worked in his firm, called Baey Kim Swee and Company.

He was a tough taskmaster, and was doing business with Korea and China at that time. We represented this company called Mannesmann, and I worked as salesman and secretary at the same time. I was an apprentice at Mannesmann for two years where, apart from being posted to the various steel mills, I was attached to the export department where I was taught the importance of export credit insurance. In fact, I would say that when Dr Goh Keng Swee wanted to start up export credit insurance and brought Dr Albert Winsemius over, the only person with any experience in that field in Singapore was me.

Anyway, after I turned eighteen, I regularly accompanied my father in his Baby Austin on business trips all the way up to Butterworth in Penang. This would have been in 1958–59. We would begin our journey in the afternoon and drive overnight to get there. The roads were really narrow in those days, and two cars passing each other would both have to slow down.

We would stop at Johor Bahru, Muar, Malacca, Seremban, Kuala Lumpur, Ipoh, Butterworth and then Penang itself.

We actually ran into tigers on the way up. You saw red eyes in the dark. Sometimes they belonged to a *seladang*, a deer. But sometimes, a tiger would be on the road.

Along the way, we would monitor what these shops were running low on, and supply them with these items, collecting payment only on our next trip. No extra charge for delivery. We stayed at $6 hotel rooms usually found on the floor above coffee shops.

We were sometimes stopped by communist guerrillas. The first time, we were carrying a lot of money with us and we lost all that. They didn't want to harm us; they just needed our involuntary donations. After that, my father would stash most of his cash somewhere in the car, and carry only small sums on his person. That way, he could pay only that and be allowed to move on. It helped that we both spoke Hokkien, I think.

After a while you got used to it.

The worst, honestly speaking, were not the communist bandits. It was the policemen. Over the years, I think we paid more to them than to the communists. The policemen would claim you were over the speed limit or had committed some other offence and ask for your driving licence. All we had to do was place $10 or so with the driver's licence before handing it over to them, and we were free to go.

Because of such experiences, I am still awed by how Lee Kuan Yew managed to stop corruption in Singapore. I did not think it at all possible. And keeping things uncorrupted is an even greater achievement.

After having lived through the Japanese occupation, I felt that we could not be subjects of others anymore, and so the appearance of the People's Action Party (PAP) under Lee Kuan

Yew in 1954 suited my sentiments fine, and I have been a supporter of the party ever since.

Anyway, I learned from my father to be very thorough in what I do. For example, when I was involved in metrication later or when fighting drug addiction, I would make sure I knew everyone involved and would leave as little to chance as possible. When Singapore was in Malaysia, I saw that there were new opportunities for our business. On my advice, Baey Kim Swee Bolts and Nuts expanded on 19 August 1964 into manufacturing, and received a pioneer certificate. Dr Goh Keng Swee, who was Minister of Finance then, was the guest of honour at the launch of the factory.

We had earlier been advised to invest in labour-intensive production. I went to Japan to get the right equipment. But soon after we joined Malaysia, it became more rational to go for higher technology in Singapore. So, we invested wrongly in the beginning, and on my bad advice. Whatever we had then, we had to move to Malaysia, where suitable labour was readily available.

I was to make a similar mistake later, when I pumped enormous sums into buying Hewlett Packard's huge Mainframe computers in the beginning of the computer era, as well as all the necessary equipment to keep the machines cool. Well, that turned out to be a bad investment, too. With the coming of small computers, these giants became useless, and we had to pay to have them carted away. Those were very bad experiences. I tend now to be among the last to go into a new trend.

I also learned the importance of humility. I used to visit iron and steel merchants in Lavender Street and Syed Alwi Road, and sometimes had to suffer insults from many of them. There was one man there whom I went to visit, hoping to sell him steel from Mannesmann. When I told him I was from Baey Kim Swee, he spat right in my face! There was bad blood between him and my father. I didn't know that. Anyway, despite my father advising me not to go back, I was determined to win the man over. So I dropped in at his place every morning, and was told to go away every time. In the end, he got tired of shouting "Get out" at me. I was soon able to sit on the chair that was in front of his desk, and was helping him to write letters and translating documents in English for him. We became friends gradually. He was my pal when he died. That was my test of humility.

Anyway, our company became a member of the Singapore Manufacturers' Association, and I was very active in it. There were many big European and American companies in Singapore then, and they had enormous factories. I became a director of Rockwell Singapore, who was here to make roller chains and control cables. Initially, the Economic Development Board had recommended me to be their local partner. They invited me to visit their factory in Holyoke, Massachusetts, for discussion. I flew there with Wong Chun Win who was my partner in another company. Representatives from EDB in the United States were also present. It was then that Mr Bailey Norton Jr, the chairman of the meeting dropped a bombshell. He told me that they had had a change of mind and would not need a local partner. I could sense that all those present expected me to burst out in anger but instead I smiled and said, "What is good for Singapore is good for me." This was in 1969, I think. That could be the reason why they invited me to be a member of their board.

I was already on the housing board then, as well as the board of the Engineering Industries Development Agency (EIDA), a supporting arm of the Economic Development Board (EDB). EIDA was started by Hon Sui Sen to provide support to various industries starting up at that time.

Partly due to Dr Goh Keng Swee's insight that shipping, fishing and tourism were the areas Singapore had to invest in, I set up three companies around this time. The first was Singapore Shipbuilding and Engineering, which was the only company in Asia at that time using something very revolutionary called synchrolifts. These made use of cradles and synchronized hoists and wenches to park giant ships on land for repairs. That way, one could actually have 100 ships lined up on land for reparation. Needless to say, this method very quickly replaced dry docks which had been the traditional way for ship repairs.

I also set up Industrial Electronic Engineering and Singapore Semiconductors. At that time, National Semiconductors (NS) had just come into the country. We became sub-contractors to them. They were the leader in the production of semiconductors in America. I was more or less a sleeping partner. The dynamic one here was Wong Chun Weng. The third person was Jimmy Chen, who joined later. We were also making products like hi-fi sets, radios and calculators. Wong was an able person and the company grew very quickly, and we even bought up Universal Electronics in Hong Kong. We also moved into China for a while, but that did not work out. The communists were not ready yet.

Souvenir Industries was the third company I started. This one did not work out well. We bought a big piece of land because we believed that creating souvenirs required inspiration, and the designers had to have peace and quiet. Things moved slowly, but in the end we did make money anyway, due solely to the appreciation in value of the land we bought.

Now, I was the chairman of all three companies, and one person I brought into Singapore Shipbuilding and Engineering was Whang Tar Liang. Tar Liang and his brother Tar Choong were owners of Lam Soon Refinery which did palm oil, and Lam Soon

Canning. They were active in Malaysia, Singapore, Hong Kong and China.

Now, Tar Liang knew Dr Goh well. The two would go on holiday cruises together with their wives. Dr Goh heard about our company, and told Tar Liang that the Minister for Defence wished to buy six sea-to-air missile boats from the German company Lürssen in Bremen-Vegesack. These would be mounted with Israeli Gabriel missiles in front and Bofors rapid-fire guns at the rear.

And so, Mindef decided to use us to purchase the boats, and in the process become a partner in the company. Until then, I was chairman of all these three companies. With this deal, I decided to hand over the chairmanship of Singapore Shipbuilding and Engineering to Tar Liang. He was the man better suited to deal with the Defence Ministry.

The plan was to buy one boat fully produced in Germany; the second would be made in Germany but assembled in Singapore; the third would be built in Singapore under Lürssen's supervision; and the last three would be built totally in Singapore by Singapore engineers and workers. The whole thing had a didactic function, obviously, and would not have happened without Mindef participation. We are talking here about superfast naval craft.

But Mindef participation meant that their people started moving in, and soon the Ministry's permanent secretary was the general manager. All of this was fine with me as long as the company continued to make money. However, it began to make losses. Don't ask me why, I really don't know how that could happen.

In short, over the years, we were arm-twisted out of Singapore Shipbuilding and Engineering, and it evolved into what is now ST Marine.

Anyway, as always, I was also interested around this time in other projects. I had been elected chairman of the engineering group of the Singapore Manufacturers Association, and I noticed many factories had lots of equipment that stood idle most of the time in their workshops. My idea was that one could start new lines of production by using these idle machines if their use was properly coordinated. So I started doing that by producing a book listing the type of equipment and facility available. To encourage more participation in this scheme, I compiled a handbook. We codified different machines because some manufacturers wanted it kept secret that they were leasing out their machines on a regular basis. It was called the Singapore Manufacturers' Handbook. A company started casting bulldozer and other heavy machinery parts and another started making motorcar and truck filters using equipment listed in the book. The idea of making products without having a factory turned out to be a success.

Dr Toh Chin Chye, who was the chairman of the PAP at that time and Deputy Prime Minister as well, heard about it, and called me up asking if it was true that such an innovation actually worked. He had received a copy of the Handbook and wanted to know more about it.

I showed him what was already being done, and he was very impressed. After that, I was invited to sit on different boards, such as the Housing & Development Board (HDB), the Ngee Ann Technical College and the Metrication Board. At Ngee Ann, I was a member of the council, together with Lim Ho Hup, the then Director of the Economic Development Board (EDB).

This was the beginning of a long journey for me as a civil servant. Since my recent retirement, I have done some sums. All in all, I spent sixty years as a chairman of statutory boards and government companies and a hundred years as a board member.

It was all voluntary work. I was not paid. I used my own car and paid for all expenses from my own pocket. I also made sure that the accounts were always properly kept. Only once did I fly on government money. That was when Hon Sui Sen, the Minister of Finance, wanted four of us to fly to the United States to study the possibility of creating a new source of supply of rice. The party comprised Lee Boon Yang, Cheng Tong Fatt, myself and the then Director of Primary Production. Thailand was being threatened by the Vietnam War spilling into Cambodia, and China would not sell to us. So, we had to go on that study trip.

Now, the HDB had Lee Hee Seng as the chairman back then. Members were Michael Fam, Victor Chew, and myself. Lim Kim San was the Minister for National Development. We did a lot back then, much of it now forgotten and unappreciated. In those days, the HDB flats were all rented out and were not properly kept. Graffiti on the walls, urine in lifts, corridors and staircases blocked, and shrubs and trees damaged. So we did our calculations and saw that the difference between rental and mortgage instalment payments was only 10–15 per cent more costly if the flats were instead sold to the applicant. The Government accepted the recommendation and overnight, the pride of ownership kept the flats in good condition.

Dr Toh warned me that when in public service, you could not afford to make a mistake: "They will throw the book at you." And if you should do well, then you may get a pat on the back and a medal. And that would be that. He was that blunt.

I had to end many of my other activities in order to be the honorary civil servant that I was to be for decades. The sad thing was my unique position upset a lot of civil servants, who did not always keep their dislike secret. This came from the fact that I could go directly to the Minister to get things done. For example, the Committee for Treatment and Rehabilitation of Drug Addicts that I had led for quite some time had its name changed to being an advisory body because of resistance from the civil service. No real meeting was held after that alteration. It was never disbanded; it was just neutralized.

THE VIETNAM CONNECTION

My father was an amazing businessman, something I repeat a lot, as you may have noticed. I remember when I was on the board of the International Trading Company (Intraco), a company started by Dr Goh Keng Swee for trade with communist countries, I found that things he taught me came in very useful in international trading.

Now, one of the most important things that my father taught me was to go where the big boys do not want to go. And where the big boys are waiting to go, you go first. The Korean War was when my father made his money. I made mine during the Vietnam War. My wife and I started a company for that, just the two of us. And the capital we started out with was actually our wedding presents. You know, jewellery and stuff. We pawned all that to use as capital.

I had seen in the newspaper that the Americans were spending more per day in Vietnam than Singapore's annual budget. There had to be money to be made there, I thought. So I decided to visit Vietnam. Now, my only connection to Vietnam at that time was through Mannesmann. I took a flight to Vietnam and got the Mannesmann representative in Saigon to drive me out to the nearest American military base. The man agreed to take me but said he wouldn't be able to bring me back. That didn't bother me. I was full of confidence in those days.

So I ended up at the gate of the camp. I asked to see the procurement officer. The guard there would not let me in, of course. But I stayed anyway and had a long chat with him, making friends with him. He was very happy talking to me. You see, the locals spoke French, not English. After quite a while, a sergeant came by with three Vietnamese to work on the roadside drain. The guard looked at me and said: "Tell you what. I'll let you go talk to the guy there. If he can't help you, then there's nothing else I can do."

That was fine by me. I went to this sergeant. He was a couple of hundred metres away. I could see that he was wearing a Freemason ring. Now, I am a Freemason as well. I had joined in 1959 or 1960 through old Forrer. So we chatted, and I was taken to the procurement office, which was manned by a Chinese who had migrated from the Mainland years ago, and had joined the army and become a lieutenant. His name was Howe. Anyway, he recommended me to one of their biggest contractors, which was a company called Pacific Architects and Engineers based in Saigon. So I went off to Saigon, met the man in charge. He was a lawyer. It so happened that he was wishing to start his own company. So I went into a joint venture with him — a 50–50 deal. This was on 11 May 1966. But that partnership ended within a year because he wanted to start supplying the American military from Thailand. So we broke up, and I suddenly found myself the sole owner of an American company — American International Industries Private Limited (AII). Unfortunately for him, Thailand wasn't really ready for that kind of production and trade. While here in Singapore, we did well. We soon obtained sufficient orders that required three 8-hour shifts with 200 staff.

We began supplying the U.S. Air Force with everything they wanted — from condoms to chickens to air-conditioners. We were supplying Bien Hoa, Phu Cat, Da Nang, Cam Ranh Bay, etc. They hadn't thought that they could buy from Singapore before that. Transporting stuff from America to the Vietnam took sixty days. So they were very happy I turned up.

Now, the first order that came in was so big that we did not have the capital to buy the necessary raw materials for production. It was for over US$2 million. They would not give letters of credit either. Payment was against invoices and shipping documents. I was used to having LCs of course, and asked for it. But that was not how they did things. I was at a loss.

Luckily, one of my sisters knew someone working at the Bank of America in Singapore. So I went to see the manager. Now, the order I received had "The United States Government Air Force" on its letterhead. I showed him the order and he exclaimed "This is as good as gold." So we got the loan we needed. Auspiciously enough, his name was Fairweather.

That same order was actually repeated twice within the next two months. It turned out that the first delivery was destroyed along the way, while the second one was cannibalized, meaning bits and pieces were taken away as spare parts by other divisions, etc.

Anyway, that was how my business with the Americans in Vietnam started. From the very beginning at AII, we had a geomancy master to advise us on our office furnishing and all sorts of other matters. That has been extremely helpful to us throughout our lives, I believe. Even today, everything in our house is placed according to *fengshui* considerations.

We supplied the Americans with everything. We were the biggest supplier in those days, using a 5,000-ton ship. A Hercules 320 would be sent for urgent deliveries. They were flown from Seletar Airport and the flight took only a day. We were securing supplies from everywhere as well. I became known for being able to supply anything.

I remember this little episode when I went with Dr Goh Keng Swee to Indonesia on an investment mission. We were told that the finance minister had a farm and Dr Goh wanted to present him with some chickens. He wanted some that would lay eggs immediately after arrival. So I told my supplier about it. The trouble was, the chickens we supplied started laying eggs on the plane and on arrival they found a consignment of chicken with eggs instead!

I was a Category Two passenger during the Vietnam War — meaning commercial personnel. I flew for free between all the air bases. I saw all those giant bases. In fact, I was the first Singaporean to actually sit in an F-5 fighter bomber. At Bien Hoa Air Base just outside Saigon, the concentration of airplanes was unimaginable. I had never, and will never again, see so many planes packed into one single airport. They were of different sizes, some armed, and mostly with wings folded upwards. Some would go up to 10 metres, some to 15 metres.

Now, the Vietcong was causing a lot of damage there. They had begun shooting hand-held rockets that would explode above the air base, sending projectiles downwards. The Air Force had so-called revetment walls which were two concrete walls filled in between with sand, but they had no roof cover. Many of the projectiles would pierce through the wings of the planes below, damaging them enough to stop them flying. The USAF called me up, asking if I could help out in some way. So I did. We constructed a double-layered expandable roof functioning like butterfly wings that could roll on the top of the revetment walls. It could be used on walls of different width. The belief was that splinters might pierce one layer, but not two. The sides were not a problem. Those were solid and protective enough. Anyway, it worked. With our new roof, we saved the planes for them and were given a testimonial by the USAF.

I was in Vietnam a lot, and as my father feared, it could get very dangerous. My wife never went, so you can imagine how worried she was all the time. For example, I was once stationed in Da Nang, in the officers' barracks. One day, I was out, having to be in Bien Hoa to get something done. A Colonel Israel called me up the next morning to tell me that the bunk where I was sleeping in Da Nang was blown up during a rocket attack the night before. Lucky me, you know. Working there could get quite dangerous. But as the business got going I employed some Americans and Australians to do the travelling. Our people were very active. We were what were called a "prime mover". In fact, the last helicopter out of Saigon had one or two of our people in it.

We got a second commendation on another occasion. The Americans had to make a lot of drops from their planes in those days, using pellets sent down with a parachute to cushion their fall. But these tended to burst apart as they hit the ground, sending whatever provisions were inside over a wide area. We actually constructed pellets for them that successfully absorbed the impact and did not break apart. This was all done by Singapore engineers. A lot of my business and ideas concerned specialized solutions, and they were often personal in that sense, requiring personal attention.

Some strange things went on there during the war. I once saw Air Force personnel roll a 44-gallon drum of oil into a drain. They didn't try to pick it up and just left it there. I was surprised and asked about it. An Air Force guy told me that it was a sort of pay-off. If they did not leave behind a drum, the Vietcong would start shooting at the tanker, destroying everything. This was an understanding they had with the enemy. You give us a bit of what you have and we leave the rest alone. It was an insurance premium, protection money. This went on all the time. Now, how do you win a war if this kind of thing is going on?

One of the colonels told me that they estimated that as much
as 30 per cent of the Vietnamese personnel working in the
airbase were Vietcong. They could not do very much about it
since they did not know who these were. This meant that the
Vietcong knew a lot about things going on in the camp.

So for three and a half years, I did this. I made my fortune.
I think it was my reputation as a supplier to the PXs (supermarkets)
in Vietnam that got Dr Goh to involve me in setting up
Mindef's SAFE Supermarket, and to have me head NTUC
Welcome as well.

GOING INTO OIL

After the war, we went into oil field supply. I left my father's
company to be on my own, and when my father died, his
hardware business went to my stepmothers. It did not thrive and
in the end I bought them out. I could afford that since the oil
field business I had gone into was doing very well. This was how
we came to own a lot of properties. But since then, the
government's compulsory acquisitions have taken most of them
off our hands. In fact, when I was on the housing board, Teh
Cheang Wan, the CEO, wanted to acquire land around Tampines.
With a stroke of his pencil on the map, my old man's 43-acre
dairy farm was gone. They paid about a million dollars for it, no
doubt, but it would be worth a billion today. At that time, my
father was still alive. He was cursing and swearing of course, and
he did not know that his son was one of the members of the
board that took all that away from him. Being young I was full of
nationalistic fervour and thought nothing of it, knowing that
the land would be used to build houses for the poor. Ironically, it
was Teh Cheang Wan who would recommend that I be appointed
a Justice of the Peace.

Now, let me talk a bit about our oil field supply business. What we do is handle the specifics of a given situation, tweaking and coming up with solutions that make the general application fit the specific case, and keeping a balance between small but decisive differences.

For example, oil rigs have this problem that some parts corrode faster than others due to variations in weathering. The side that faces the wind, for example, will wear away faster than the side that is away from it. We came up with three products — Americote, Americhem and Ameripad. The first is coated with a special type of paint that is corrosion resistant. You cannot be using high-quality stainless steel everywhere, so the solution is to have a coat that will protect the threads of the nuts and bolts and other parts from corroding too early.

Now, you can design anything you like, but no one will believe you without you holding seminars and exhibitions and showing potential customers how reliable your products are. So we did all that — in Malaysia and Indonesia and elsewhere. All this cost a lot of money. We would use our products on chosen projects for free, so that the customer could see them tested against rust and then compare them with competitors. This would be done over six-month periods.

We did the same with water treatment and industrial chemicals as well. The product is named Americhem. In big boilers, for example, there are parts that rust and clog up, and turn inefficient. So, like in the case of the Krakatau Steel Mill started by the Russians in Indonesia, we let them use our chemicals for free for six months, and after that, they could see for themselves how well corrosion had been kept at bay. After that, we got a contract for a year or two.

Our third product in this business is Ameripad. This solves a problem that no common person even imagines exists. This one was actually my son Henry's idea, and we developed it in Singapore. Now, oil pipelines can stretch for thousands and thousands of miles over very difficult terrain. They are placed on concrete and sometimes wood "saddles" as they are called. Long pipelines tend to be on concrete, and are coated to protect them from the elements. Steel pipelines contract and expand as temperatures change, and that is allowed for in the construction. But there is one spot that takes more punishment than anywhere else, and that is where the pipe rests on the saddle. Here, the rubbing wears down the wall of the pipe, and that is where you begin to have leakages. Replacing the pipes will incur enormous cost not to mention stoppage of delivery of the oil, and we are talking about very isolated areas. What we came up with was Ameripad, a cushion you put between the pipe and the saddle. This specialized product is anti-corrosive and it softens the rubbing as well, thus prolonging the life of the pipelines. One of these costs a few dollars and although huge quantities are used, the savings for the customer are substantial.

My son Charles managed a factory in Kerteh, Trengganu. There were significant innovations that we did there as well. For example, when you coat a steel plate or a ship hull or an oil rig, you have to make sure the surface is clean. In the old days, sand was used to blast the surface clean. But sand particles getting into the lungs of workers caused serious illness, so that was banned. What we did instead was to use slag from copper foundries which was crushed and sorted into different sizes and grades.

I don't mean to sound ostentatious, but this is what entrepreneurship is. Innovativeness is what it is. We innovate for specific purposes, and we fill in the gaps and solve problems that seem small but where the damage is significant. This is our niche. Few people invest in developing such products. It costs too much. But once you have done that, everyone wants to copy and get in on the act. So we have a lot of imitations to deal with, and we had to introduce a traceability process for our little nuts and bolts. Each bolt is traceable to its origin, and a guarantee for free replacement for defects is given. Patents do not always help. You just have to keep ahead, provide good service and good quality products. In any industry, one has to look intensely at things, and you are bound to see something that can be improved, or some need that the major players just do not have time to look into and are merely making do with temporarily. There are always such things around. Generally, people are blind to these, mainly because they have not taught themselves to see them.

We also introduced pumps for use in oil production rigs which are cheaper and more durable than the ones being used earlier. After much testing, we are now a major supplier of these, with servicing included. Esso has large numbers of oil rigs and Shell alone has over 200 rigs in the region, so our people are running around endlessly, servicing them. Our managing staff in Singapore numbers about a hundred. We have just closed our Russia office since I am now too old to handle it and my sons do not want to go there.

My dealings with the Soviet Union and Russia began when I set up an office in Moscow during the Mikhail Gorbachev years, in 1986. Later, we had one in Kiev as well. We also had an office in Teheran. A former senior staff of EDB told me he had good connections in Iran. The plan was to export steel and equipment from our Russia operation but things didn't work out. So we closed the Teheran office after one year in operation.

I also learned that the Russians trusted American businessmen and the name of American International Industries was good for business. Because of a deal I made with this Russian who was the head of the Zabaikalsh Railway, which connected Russia to China, I came to practically monopolize the railway transport. The town

on the Chinese side is called Manzhouli. Now, with the fall of the
Soviet Union, Moscow was short of coke and coal. So we ended
up bringing in Chinese coke and coal to Russia and selling
Russian steel to China. Russia was dealing a lot in iron and steel,
and most of this was exported by sea to the rest of the world.
I was the only one using rail. That made it so much cheaper to
transport. I was making a lot of money, and I got all sorts of offers
from Russians seeking my help for all sorts of transactions.
For example, the MIG-29 deal between the Russian and Malaysian
governments was arranged by us. But I ended up not being paid
the commission promised. There was a later case that involved
Brunei. That time, I demanded that the Russian government paid
2 per cent as commission in advance for any military equipment
they wanted us to push. That made the negotiator very angry.
But since he was not going to agree, I refused to go further into
the matter.

Seriously, doing business in Russia was very difficult, even
though our company was registered as Russian. I had on my
payroll someone who was involved with the growing mafia
menace there. What I learned from him about these people was
that they would go to a bank manager and demand to be given
a list of foreign companies with U.S. dollar accounts at the bank.
Should the manager refuse to give it, he would be shot on the
spot. Needless to say, bank managers soon began giving out these
lists. With these lists, the mafia could then intimidate and blackmail
the foreign companies. This same person disappeared one day
without any trace after stepping out from his home. According to
his wife, he didn't even take along his car key or wallet.

What we usually did was to bring in cash. When a payment
was due, I would go into Russia with large sums of cash. My chaps
would arrange with the military to provide security escort to our
office where payment to the supplier was made immediately.

The mafia was so bold in those days they would battle military guards. I saw a really serious shooting battle once outside a supermarket across the road from our office that had refused to pay them. After the gun battle, there were a lot of bullet holes on the nearby buildings. I was told what had happened to an electronics shop that would not pay up either. They had a rocket shot right through the shop.

About seven or eight years ago, I went to Sakhalin for a preliminary meeting with Mobil. They were looking for a Russian company to set up a facility to thread drill pipes there. After I gained a letter of intent from them, I flew to Houston to meet up with an experienced engineering manager to manage the workshop. Our Russian staff in Moscow had agreed to take care of the rest.

Now, the seas around Sakhalin are frozen six months of the year. The temperature can go down to −45°C and the snow can pile up as high as the second storey of buildings overnight.

Mobil had the rig on land and the plan was to drill horizontally 18 kilometres into the sea where the oil deposit was. They planned to operate simultaneously, ten parallel horizontal drills! Inside the oil rig was ambient temperature but our workshop's temperature could go down to as low as −45°C. The alternative to setting up the workshop was to send broken parts to Japan, and that would be too costly.

I flew there many times to lease the required land and sought quotations for building the workshop. I fell sick each time I arrived there and I knew that the weather was too much for me. My two sons were quite happy managing the business in Singapore and did not wish to go. So, in the end, despite it being a gold mine, I had to give it up. Finally, we closed down our operations in Russia.

I had properties in Moscow that I had earlier bought in my wife's name. They were sold at a loss. To our chagrin, we learned that women had a low standing in property ownership under Russian law. I had sent my wife to Moscow to dispose of our properties and although she was stated as the owner in the title documents, she was not permitted to sell them without the approval of her husband. The end result was that I had to go to give my official approval in person and that was when I fell sick again.

In any case, I think our business will still be mainly oilfield supply related for some time to come. Oil is still king. My journey from nuts and bolts to oilfields supply has a simple logic in the end. Oil rigs are held in place with nuts and bolts. Having reliable nuts and bolts can save the oil companies a lot of money.

After I became fully involved in public services, I left things to my brother-in-law at first, then to my brother. When I felt my eldest son Henry was ready, I brought him back to run things from Singapore. He was sent to Brunei after he got his degree in Business Administration in the United States. Things were in a mess there, and he did very well in turning things around. After that I moved him back to run things centrally in Singapore, although I remained as chairman. In Brunei, we could only work with local established companies.

Our company is still known as American International Industries (AII) Group of Companies although it is now wholly owned by my family. We have offices in many countries — in Germany, in Russia, in Malaysia, and elsewhere. It is our policy to reinvest our profit overseas. This is because profit made elsewhere is not subject to Singapore tax if they are not brought in. We have retained the name because it is now so well known, it would be too much trouble changing it.

We are located mainly in countries where there are oil fields. We have a factory in Kerteh in Trengganu, for example. There is an office in Kuala Lumpur, as well. In fact, we have been there for over 40 years. We could only work through joint ventures in Malaysia because of the *bumiputera* policy. We had a number of offices there, even in Sabah and Sarawak.

Our early partners in Malaysia were extremely nice people — royalty from Perak and Kedah: Raja Zainal and Tunku Zaidah. I had known them for a very long time. As a young businessman working for my father, I hung out with Raja Zainal and his friends at The Spotted Dog — that was what we used to call the Royal Selangor Club. They were such trustworthy people. At that time, we operated under Raja Zainal's name. It so happened that both the husband and wife drowned in a boat accident to our great shock and sorrow. They had a huge family, with lot of siblings and half-siblings, but no children. I was afraid that we would lose everything that we had owned under his name. However, a month after Raja Zainal's death, his safe was opened and his will was read. In it was mentioned a list of all the companies that actually belonged to me. He willed his relatives to make certain that these were all returned to "my good friend, Baey Lian Peck".

How often do you meet such honest people?

We were in Germany as well. Before the oil crisis of 1973, I believe that there were five large diesel engine plants in the world, manufacturing engines that were 5 megawatts and above. Finland had one and Germany had four, one of which became ours. Everything was on an enormous scale. This was after the fall of the Berlin Wall. I already had a small company in Germany at that time, and when the Government put one of the East German plants up for sale, I tendered and managed to get it. This was in the state of Halberstadt. There were a lot of incentives from the government at that time, one of which was for research and development.

Anyway, we were making money but it was because of these subsidies and because of the greed of the leadership of the union, IG Metall, that we were forced into liquidation. According to the agreement with the German government for research grants, any design invention had to be kept in Germany for five years, after which I could do whatever I liked with it. My plan was to set up a similar company in Singapore once the five years were over.

We were employing about 200 engineers then. Our brilliant chief engineers and I — with experience from my days at the Metrication Board — managed to design and build a prototype revolutionary engine with about 9,000 instead of the traditionally 20,000 and more parts which promised to make repairs relatively easy. Tests showed that our modular cylinder system engine could cut breakdown time from two weeks to two days. We exhibited the engine very successfully at the Hanover Industrial Fair 2000. It turned out to be a mistake to let it out too early. The union heard about it and wanted to take over. I was warned that there were plans to steal our technical drawings. So my son Charles and I took the computer's hard discs that contained the design to another state, to Magdeburg. Anyway, they got to know we had taken the plans out of the factory, and accused us of taking them to Singapore, which would have been illegal. Now, why would I invest 40–50 million deutsche mark and then do something stupid like that? In any case, they came on a Sunday without a warrant and sealed up the factory. They also came to my house without a warrant, four burly, huge German policemen with an interpreter. They forced their way in at around 7.00 pm and searched our home for about two hours while my wife and I stood by and watched. Had they told me what they were looking for, I would have helped them. But they didn't.

The Member of Parliament for Halberstadt was the union adviser. It was all very big news, and all the major news media published daily about the stolen engine design. You see, all but one of the ministers in the state were union appointees, including the chief minister. The man who had supported our investment was Minister Gabriel, the former mayor of Halberstadt where our factory was located. The German company MBH had an in-house power plant and had long-term contracts to supply power to neighbouring homes and supermarkets. Being locked out of the office and factory, it was compelled to seek judicial protection for temporary liquidation. Later, one of my former employees told me that it was published in *Die Spiegel*, a well-known magazine, that Minister Gabriel was sacked a few months later.

I wrote to the Minister for Finance in the German federal government, but the reply was that they could not intervene since the states had autonomy in such matters. That was part of the Germany merger agreement. The company had sold its factory land and buildings to Singapore for 100 million deutsche mark financing. The sales were legally registered with the authority and title deeds (Deutscher Grundschuldbrief) issued but the receiver nevertheless claimed that the sale and transfer was not legal.

We went to court, and that court was also in Halberstadt, and we lost. At that time, the factory was worth well over 100 million deutsche mark. We lost it, just like that.

We were already on the verge of listing our German factory on the Singapore stock exchange. We had made a profit of about 1.5 million deutsche mark. A 10 per cent swop of shares had been agreed to with Kian Ann Engineering, a Singapore company listed in SGX. The Overseas Union Bank had agreed to underwrite up to 25 per cent of the shares to be issued. It was at this crucial stage that the policemen, instigated by the IG Metall, sealed our factory.

When doing business internationally, everything depends on contacts. Not even your own government can help you. I wrote to H.E. Walter Woon, the Singapore Ambassador to Germany. Not so much as a reply came back.

If you go on the Internet today, you can still see the company there. It is called Maschinenbau Halberstadt. I was the chairman and owner of that company. My son-in-law owned half of it, and I the other half. But they engineered the liquidation of the company. You see, when a factory stops running, the overhead piles up very quickly. So after six months, they said the company was bankrupt, and had debts of 200 million deutsche mark. And that was that. This was in 2004. What I learned from this was that if you have a huge manufacturing business in a foreign country, it is advisable to have the government involved, or to have union support.

There are always risks in business. The more lucrative it is and the more profit you think you can make; the more risks you are bound to be taking. My business philosophy is I do not venture my capital. I use whatever profit I have made as the risk capital. That was what I have normally done. There must always be a buffer.

Business is also based on experience — experience that builds up your gut feeling. This cannot be transferred through words, either verbally or in written form. For example, in Russia, they must booze after a contract is signed. So we learned to do that. After a signing, we would move to another room and have drinks. We would become very good friends through that, and new contracts would follow.

Chapter 2

SEEKING TO SERVE

I am therefore basically a businessman, and, fortunately, I gained financial success very early in life. So, from thirty-eight years old onwards, a lot of my time went into serving Singapore, and I could do that without ever taking payment for my work for the government.

This was my national service.

I think my commitment to work for the country came when Lee Kuan Yew cried on the air, when Singapore was kicked out of Malaysia in 1965. After the Japanese Occupation, we had all felt that we had to become independent. Either you chose to migrate or you stayed to fight. My old man and I actually discussed that, and we decided to stay.

Lee Kuan Yew took us into the federation in 1963, and at that time, I remember I didn't agree with him. But I soon saw that he was learning, and changing his policies accordingly. After that, I was all for him. I remember Dr Toh Chin Chye asking me to enter politics. He could not guarantee that I would become a Minister, but a position of Minister of State was a foregone conclusion. I said no to him. I saw myself as a businessman. My father taught me things as a businessman, and we had always been doing business. Certain things you may do in business which you cannot do in politics. In business, you make use of the grey areas. One gets involved in what used to be called "yellow culture", for example. I mean, I was doing business with the Americans in Vietnam. I knew who did what to whom, and when.

Politics is something else altogether. So, I did not want to discredit the party. That was my official excuse to Dr Toh. But in truth, I did not want to. It was as simple as that.

Years later, after my work with NTUC Welcome, Lim Kim San also wanted me to join politics. I turned him down too, and for the same reason. To be sure, I became a cadre for the PAP in 1971. I was on too many important boards to not be one, I suppose. Although I stopped being a cadre later, I remained a member of the PAP. So I knew the top leaders very well. I knew Devan Nair very well. We were good personal friends and I kept no secrets from them. They knew I was a Freemason. Now, there are American friends of mine who like to class Singapore as a dictatorship — a benevolent one, they would add. But the truth is, no dictatorship tolerates Freemasons.

I agreed to run organizations for the ministries, and knowing how the two worlds were different, I made sure I never took a cent for myself, and I kept meticulous accounts of everything I did that involved expenditures. The cost of coffees, stamps, stationery and other items used by me or my visiting friends were duly accounted and paid for at the end of each month. I still have these expenditure books with me.

My first appointment within the government was as board member in the Housing & Development Board (HDB), a statutory board. I was quite excited about that position, and eagerly set out to learn as much as I could about running a board meeting. There was a new chairman, Lee Hee Seng. He was the managing director of Singapura Building Society, and had been a housing board member since 1966 and becoming chairman only in 1971. He was a smooth chairman. He was never known to lose his temper, and he was always full of understanding for others. Yet, he was very firm. I actually studied the man closely, and even noted down everything he did which I thought I should imitate. I didn't think of it then, but he was my teacher, a very impressive man. It was from him I learned what we call parliamentary procedure in the board room. I am glad that I had the opportunity to tell him recently that I learned a lot from him, and that he was a pillar of strength for me in those days.

SINGAPORE METRICATION BOARD (1971–1981)

The Metrication Board was one of my first involvements with government work. Now, metrication was more important to our nation building than most people think. By 1970, as much as 90 per cent of the world's inhabitants in 120 countries lived under the metric system of weights and measure. More vitally, 60 per cent of the gross national product of the world was produced in metric.

One can see that it was necessary for Singapore to do likewise, and to do so as quickly and smoothly as possible. After all, by 1969, 90 per cent of Singapore's external trade was with countries that were either already using the metric system or committed to conversion to the system. Of Singapore's major trading partners, apart from Hong Kong and Brunei, only the United States had not decided to go metric.

Even Commonwealth countries were beginning to go metric, and together with other factors such as the opportunity to rationalize industrial and engineering practices, exercise modular co-ordination in the building industry, and benefit from the experience of others and avoiding higher costs as the economy developed, there were good reasons for us to follow suit.

Singapore was using three systems of weights and measures back then. The British imperial system was of course the accepted norm, alongside the local customary system involving the *chupak, gantang, kati, tahil* and *pikul*, which was popular in the retail trade. The metric system was used in specialized areas such as electrical engineering and in the teaching of science.

Being decimally based, the metric system had a great advantage over the others, and standardization around such a system would greatly benefit the wholesale and retail trade.

It was already announced in Parliament in December 1968 that Singapore would go metric, and that the Ministry of Science and Technology would study the implications and submit to the government proposals for necessary legislative adjustments and implement whatever administrative innovations were required.

In November 1970, the ministry submitted a White Paper to Parliament for adoption, titled "A Report on a Study of the Proposed Conversion to the Metric System in Singapore". Two Bills resulted from this, both of which were passed on 15 February 1971. The first was the Metrication Bill (1970), which introduced the International System (SI Systeme International d'Unites) of weights and measures, and the second was the Weights and Measures (Amendments) Bill legalizing the use of SI units.[1]

On 13 December that year, the Metrication Board was set up, and I was named chairman. We were neither a statutory board nor a department in the ministry. Since we knew we had to have an integrated approach, the board included people from all the key chambers of commerce, the major bodies for Singapore's architects, engineers, surveyors and manufacturers, the Consumers Association of Singapore (CASE), the National Trades Union Congress (NTUC) and the Singapore Institute of Standards and

Industrial Research (SISIR). We divided ourselves into five main committees — Economic, Education, Publicity, Technical and Tertiary Education (including Industrial Training) Committees.

We must have held thousands of meetings. If you talked about furniture, you had to get furniture manufacturers together; and if you talked about retailers, you had to get those together. The committees met, and then issues were brought to the board for deliberation. I made sure that we were very meticulous with the minutes of these meetings. I think the National Archives are filled with thousands of minutes from these meetings.

I remember going on a study trip in February 1972 to Japan, the United States and the United Kingdom. In London, I visited the U.K. Metrication Board to learn about the effects of metrication on trade and industry, and to discuss how children could be educated in the metric system and how best to prepare the public for the switch. Japan had gone metric by then, while the implications of metrication were being studied in the United States. The United Kingdom was halfway through its decade-long conversion programme.

Our timing for this major reform was not the best, given the global recession that began in January 1973 and which was worsened by the jump in petroleum prices orchestrated by the Organization of the Petroleum Exporting Countries (OPEC) in October 1973. Nevertheless, it was decided that the public sector would go metric by the end of 1975, at which time, 75 per cent of the industrial sector should be using the new measurements. Progress was most obvious in the engineering industry, where 40 per cent of firms had by July 1974 gone fully metric and another 35 per cent had attained metric capacity.

The public sector would set the pace of metrication, since any change in the government departments and statutory bodies would affect the population in varying degrees. This would gear the public towards the shift. For instance while metrication in the Central Supplies Office affected only the suppliers, the adoption of metric units by the Public Utilities Board in the billing of water, gas and electricity affected almost the entire population. And so, by taking the lead in metrication, the public sector paved the way for the private sector to follow.

We acted as co-ordinator for metrication in the public sector, and government departments and statutory bodies were requested to submit details of their metrication programmes for the Board's study and approval. For example, the HDB took the lead by using metric in all their plans for new housing estates. This of course motivated the rest of the building industry to metricate. And in mid-1974, the Building Control Division made it obligatory for architects to submit their plans with metric specifications if they wished for speedy approval. In real estate, the public sector and the Singapore Land and Building Developers' Association agreed to exclusive metrication in all promotional and sales literature with effect from January 1979.

Generally, all the industries supported metrication once they were convinced that it was inevitable and at the same time advantageous to them. The speed at which metrication could be introduced in the various industries depended very much on the policies and developments of parent companies overseas and on the management of local companies. For instance, metrication in the oil rig building industry made very little impact because major rig building firms then were America-based. At the same time, many industrial firms were either using metric system already or were capable of handling metric designs. About 10 per cent still engaged in imperial production due to customer requirements. Similarly, more than 90 per cent of large shipbuilding and repairing yards were already metricated.

Metrication in the civil aviation industry was slow. This was mainly because of two factors — the danger of human errors costing lives during the transitional period, and the sluggishness of international regulatory bodies.

Things were more complicated and sensitive where the retail trade was concerned. "Sale by Retail" is defined in the Weights and Measures Act 1975 as "a sale to a person buying for his own use or consumption". This meant normal outlets, i.e. supermarkets, emporiums, departmental stores, provision shop and markets.

Now, the metrication of the retail trade involved a chain reaction running from foreign exporters through the importers and wholesalers to retailers and finally to the customers. The use of three systems of measurement had always caused confusion among consumers, and many retailers tried to discourage support for metrication among their clients. We decided to tackle this by beginning with voluntary conversion and then moving on to a mandatory changeover.

Now, goods that are sold by retail come in two forms, namely, pre-packed or loose. "Pre-packed" means goods made up in advance and ready for sale in a container in either standard or non-standard sizes, and "loose" means goods weighed or measured out in the required quantity in the presence of the buyer. Thus, the retail sale of a particular item can be conducted in either one of these two methods or both. For example, rice can be sold in the provision shops in standard sizes of 500 g, 1 kg, 3 kg, 6 kg, and 10 kg packs, or loose; while butter can only be sold in standardized packs of 10 g, 125 g, 250 g, and 500 g.

Pre-packed goods can be divided into two categories, namely, quantity critical and quantity non-critical. The first includes products that are consumed in substantial quantities where the buyer is likely to be more concerned about the unit prices and the amount he is getting. Examples are edible oils, rice and sugar. For such products, it is essential to get standard metric sizes for consumer protection. These sizes must be the only sizes available at retail outlets so that no unfair advantages can be taken by packaging goods in slightly smaller sizes.

In the quantity non-critical category, the buyer is not concerned with the quantity he is getting as the purchase is often determined by the quality or brand. Buyers in this category seldom make comparisons of unit prices, and it would suffice to have the contents "soft" or directly converted to metric units.

Now, metrication of quantity critical items had to be preceded by standardization and rationalization. To complete the metrication exercise, "blanket" legislation was introduced to ensure that all pre-packed goods carried metric labelling and were packed in agreed standardized sizes. The trick was to balance consumer interest not only with the ability of the manufacturers to metricate but more importantly, with ultimate benefit to both parties through metrication. Take cooking oil for example. Prior to metrication, this item was being sold in thirty-six different sizes and quantities, believe it or not. Rival brands packed in gallons, fluid ounces, pounds, litres, kilograms and *kati*. The diversity in sizes and quantities caused considerable confusion for the buyers and was uneconomical for suppliers, since they were forced to carry a wide range of stocks. We actually managed to standardize and rationalize the sizes into a metric range of six, enabling the manufacturers to reduce their container inventories and increase production. And with standardized packaging, consumers could easily compare the worth of their purchases.

Knowing that resistance or lethargy would be greatest in the retail markets, we decided to implement the changes in stages. The first involved textile retail. This was started in March 1972 but progress was slow. I had to give a public assurance that metrication was not leading to higher prices. One problem to be dealt with was the practice of "rounding up" in the switch from yard to metre. What we did was to construct conversion tables that rounded downwards instead. On 1 August 1972, with sponsorship from the Chartered Bank, we made available two special booklets where this was applied — *Metric Conversation Tables* and *SI for the Layman.*

One major innovation that I am personally proud of was the reconstruction of the *daching.* This traditional Chinese weighing instrument adopted for use in Malaysia and Singapore had been severely criticized for the possibility it gave a retailer to cheat. For example, the "counterweight" could be easily replaced with a lighter one; the calibration was not visible to the buyer and the bar hung oblique when the fulcrum was at the correct point. Court cases involving the misuse of the *daching* and of faulty *daching* were plentiful in Singapore and had been so throughout its history.

We were sure that any attempt to replace this traditional tool with the saucer scale would meet with serious objection, especially from Chinese retailers and consumers. So I went to see Professor E. A. Burges at the Department of Engineering, University of Singapore. I wanted him to design for us "a fool-proof, non-cheating *daching*" where the correct measure would be reflected by the bar being horizontal, the calibration being visible to the consumer and the counterweight being irremovable.

We suspected that retailers would opt for the "saucer scale" once the cheating features of the traditional *daching* had been removed.

In April 1972, while attending a four-day Commonwealth conference on metrication in London, I advertently made the disclosure that a metric *daching* was being devised to replace the traditional model. At the same time, I arranged for over 20,000 saucer scales to be imported and announced that all weighing scales must now be of these approved types. Making sure the two would cost the same, retailers were offered the choice between using the metric non-cheating *daching* or the saucer scale. As we expected, most of them opted for the saucer scale. This scale is easier to use then the cumbersome new metric *daching* that had furthermore been stripped of all the "advantages" to the retailer. Thus the traditional Chinese *daching* died a natural death in Singapore without any legislation.

On 1 July 1974, major supermarkets in Singapore went metric in their sale of frozen goods, led by Cold Storage, Fitzpatrick's, Greatways, Tay Buan Guan, Supreme and NTUC Welcome. This marked the second stage in our efforts to leave old scales behind, be they British or Chinese.

Not all industries were as co-operative. We noticed by August 1974 that textile shops were behaving rather indifferently to metrication, and were still importing and selling by the yard. This worrying development was fuelled by a global trend: countries that were metricating fast were off-loading their old instruments onto countries that were more sluggish in this process. This led the Singapore Government to place licensing restrictions on the import of weighing and measuring instruments that were scaled in imperial units.

At the same time, retailers were digging in and were waiting for legislation to be passed before they would go metric. This was an irritant for me. I was after all trying my best to avoid using force. In fact, the gradualism that I preferred was causing worry in certain quarters. On 19 March 1975, for example, Dr Toh Chin Chye had to parry a query put to him in Parliament by P. Govindaswamy on the slow speed at which metrication was taking place. The preferred method, Dr Toh argued, echoing me, was "gradual and painless". It was tough going for a while.

A survey in 1975 showed that as many as 52 per cent of housewives, especially those above 44 years old, had no knowledge of the simplest metric units such as "metre" and "kilogram". There were two areas, however, where we decided against metricating. One was where property and land were concerned, and the other was in the sale of Chinese medicines. The former involved leases and contracts stretching over long periods of time, and it was thought best to leave that alone. New contracts were, however, obligated to use metric measures. Chinese medicines are sometimes sold in extremely small quantities, and it was thought risky to intervene in this calibration.

In December 1975, I publicly advised manufacturers and packagers to "metricate for survival". I told them that the standardization and rationalization of sizes would mean considerable savings in inventory and storage space. At the same time, I warned that any exploitation of public ignorance and confusion would lead to powers found in the Weights and Measures Act being enforced.

We had two publications to educate the public, manufacturers, retailers and industrialists. Over a period, about 200,000 copies of *The Metric Way* came out each month in English and Chinese and were distributed by the HDB to its residents. *The Metric Digest* was only in English and was meant for industrial and commercial sectors.

While I preferred a gradual process, I knew that legislation would be necessary if the agreed standard sizes that all concerned parties had worked so hard to achieve were to be respected. Without legislation, regression, even if by a recalcitrant minority, was inevitable. Without legislation, the board's function would deteriorate to one of policing.

In July 1979, we began to introduce laws on retail trade metrication. Later that year, I made an announcement that metrication in Singapore was nearing its end, and the commerce, industry and service sectors had already completed the change. Where the retail trade was concerned, further regulations on margarine, edible oils, milk power and powered detergent were soon to be implemented.

It was on 31 December 1981 that the Singapore Metrication Board was dissolved, after eleven years of existence. On the whole, the process had been quite painless. I think the decision to implement the policy in stages, patiently and with central control was what assured its success. Government bodies set the example by being the first to go metric; wholesalers and manufacturers were targeted next; and then retailers and consumers.

The measure of our success wasn't whether or not metric conversion got done, but whether it caused disruption and dislocation in the process. It would also be based on whether the conversion brought economic benefits to the country. I can proudly say that we were quite successful in both these respects.

NTUC FAIRPRICE (1973-1982)

It was in mid-June 1973 that the first cooperative supermarket in Singapore came into being. This was at Toa Payoh, and it was started by a new cooperative society called NTUC Welcome Consumers' Co-operative Limited. To be sure, the society was already registered on 14 March that year. This was the country's third cooperative venture, all initiated by the National Trades Union Congress. The other two were NTUC Income, which took care of insurance, and NTUC Comfort, which ran a taxi service. All these were ideas that stemmed from Dr Goh Keng Swee, the Minister for Defence.

Now, the idea behind NTUC Welcome was to limit the profiteering practices of shopkeepers, which as you can imagine becomes quite unacceptable during inflationary times. Welcome Development Organisation had been started under the chairmanship of NTUC's president Phey Yew Kok, and its board of trustees had my old friend Lim Kim San, the Minister for Environment, as chairman. Devan Nair, who was also a friend of mine, was deputy chairman. He was also secretary-general of NTUC Although I was still chairman of the Metrication Board at the time, Lim Kim San called me in to chair NTUC Welcome's board, with Phey as my deputy chairman. From the beginning, Lim Kim San wanted me to fight inflation, and even make money if possible. Our initial capital was supposed to be $1 million, with provisions for up to $10 million. But Kim San offered me only $250,000 as a start. I remember laughing at him: "Do you think I am a miracle worker?"

But I took it on, and we actually succeeded. I knew that fighting inflation under those circumstances was not going to be easy. Ideas are a dime a dozen, but getting things done is something else. So I had to learn about the retail business really fast, and in a way very unlike how I engaged retailers during the metrication process.

My plan was to keep the prices of a dozen or so basic items low. I succeeded in that. When I left nearly ten years later, the price of rice, for example, was cheaper than when I first joined.

But prices *were* going wild in 1973. Now, Singapore being what it is, we could not adopt price controls. What I thought we could do instead was to cross-subsidize our items. My idea was to use profits made from non-basic items to subsidize the prices of basic items. At the same time, I had to make sure that whatever drop in price I succeeded in making would not be too sudden or too substantial. That would upset wholesalers and retailers and disturb market mechanisms too much. So, we had to do our calculations most carefully.

Since our official goal was to fight inflation, we expected to have a hard time getting supplies from the big wholesalers controlling the market. They would see us as people trying to undermine their business. I told Kim San as much, and he went to tell that to Prime Minister Lee Kuan Yew. So, already at the launching of NTUC Welcome on 22 July 1973, Prime Minister Lee openly warned suppliers against discriminating against the co-operative: "Any wholesaler who withholds popular or fashionable goods in great demand from this co-op supermarket, to give it to his pet detail network, will be bucking not only the labour movement but also the Government. Any goods found in any other supermarket can and will be found in this supermarket, if buyers want them."[2]

What I did then was to bring a cut-out of the report of his speech along with me whenever I went to wholesalers to source for things. That did help, but then, these people wanted payment in cash. So I had to negotiate with them. They finally agreed to a sixty-day credit but at their normal price. Now, how were we to fight inflation if our purchase prices were controlled by these people?

At that time, I was on the board of Intraco, another brainchild of Dr Goh's. This was formed to trade with Eastern bloc countries, so we had a lot of dealings with them at the time. Intraco — International Trading Company — comprised of three parts representing Government, Industry and Commerce. Being manager of Bolts and Nuts and being a member of the Singapore Manufacturers Association, I was there as a founder-member representing Industry.

Now, Phey, being the NTUC president, didn't like the idea of being my deputy at Welcome. I remember chairing the first Welcome board meeting, and of course I applied everything I had learned from watching Lee Hee Seng at HDB. That riled Phey up no end for some reason, and he swore at me in Hokkien. He was quite a rough and tough fellow. Anyway, he insisted that the aim of NTUC Welcome must be to benefit members of the union.

I did not agree, and said that I was appointed by the Minister, and my job was to guard the interests of Singaporeans in general, not those of the union. He became very angry at that, and decided to set up his own supermarket network. It was called SILO/PIEU, a joint venture between the Singapore Industrial Labour Union and the Pioneer Industries Employees Union. Wherever we set up an outlet, SILO/PIEU would do the same. I told Devan Nair about the situation, and he said to give Phey enough rope and he would hang himself. I remember I was in London for the Commonwealth Metrication Conference when my general manager called to tell me that Phey, who was also a PAP MP, was starting his own chain, and wanted us to purchase stocks for him. I replied that we could do that, but only in the way any running business establishment would do. We would have to add a couple of percent in commission, and he would have to pay cash. We would not be able to extend him any free credit. Phey became even angrier with me. He started his chain nevertheless, and so Welcome had to compete against SILO/PIEU.

As part of the country's food security measure, Welcome was allowed to import rice. We bought hundreds of tonnes of rice and other basic items to supply the shops for the whole of Singapore. Enormous amounts. This was a risky matter, for two reasons. Firstly, prices fluctuated greatly, and secondly the temptation to take bribes or kickbacks was very high. The Thai businessmen were experts at arranging inappropriate kickbacks.

You can imagine how great the temptation could be for someone who might be in serious need of money. There was no one to keep tabs on you. We are talking here about millions of dollars every month. I told my vice-chairman that we had to be very cautious, as this rice importing business could be our downfall. Now, when I heard that Phey and SILO/PIEU were also getting into the act, and that he was flying off to Thailand to buy huge quantities of rice for import, I knew that that could be the end of him. True enough, he was charged with four counts of criminal breach of trust in December 1979. He jumped bail though, and escaped the country and hasn't been heard from since. It was after Phey ran off that Welcome took over SILO/ PIEU, ending about six years of competition. That was what Lim Kim San wanted, and Devan Nair as well. That was how NTUC FairPrice came into being, with that merger.

Now the name "FairPrice" was actually my coinage, although the name change came just around the time I left Welcome. I was in Dhaka in Bangladesh on a trade mission one day, and was feeling poorly. I needed to get medication and was taken to a drug store. That drug store was fortunately called "Fair Price". It clicked in my head that that was the right name for us. You see, we did not have enough outlets in the beginning, and we were hoping to mobilize normal provision shops in every street to carry our essential items. We had to make these easily accessible to the common people. All in all, there were about ten or twelve such items. Most provision shop owners are Chinese, and they would feel that with a sign in front of their shops saying that their prices were fair — *kong toh* in Hokkien — their reputation would grow. So I felt that the name should be popular with them and should induce them to join us and carry our goods.

In the beginning, you would see long queues coming to buy essential items from us particularly rice and sugar. The prices of these essential items were purposely reduced to attract customers. They were called "loss leaders". As expected, most of the hawkers who sold *nasi lemak* or chicken rice and similar food stalls, were also attracted to them. These two items were placed at the back of the supermarket so that customers would be enticed to buy other things along the way.

The OPEC oil crisis had just begun. Oil prices jumped ten times and Singapore being dependent almost entirely on import, food prices went up overnight by over 200 per cent. The task of keeping inflation low became extremely necessary particularly on essential items.

In a supermarket, we would have 8,000 to 10,000 items ranging from perfumes to milk powder and baby food. When I first studied the problem, it certainly looked insurmountable. The rice market, for example, was controlled by four or five importers who were supplying various items not only to Singapore but also to Malaysia, Thailand, Indonesia and the Philippines. These were the big guys with turnovers of hundreds of millions of dollars. And this was 30 years ago.

Keeping the price of daily necessities low is vital for an average family. As I said earlier, the essential food that a Singaporean family needs are rice, sugar, salt, cooking oil, milk powder, chicken, fish and others totalling about a dozen items. When these essential items on which the cost of living index is based are keep reasonable low, there is no pressure for workers to demand higher pay. This has a chain reaction effect on the economy. It is when workers' wages are kept lower than those in competing countries that foreign investors find it more attractive to invest in Singapore.

Selling most of the items at prices comparable to that of other retailers would ensure that we did not run the provision shops out of business. This would have happened if we had been selling at prices clearly lower than theirs. Our strategy was to keep only twelve items of daily necessities cheaper at NTUC Welcome.

The *Straits Times* article of 11 September 1978 under the heading "Singapore checks inflation's rise" bears testimony to the success of our strategy. It read: "latest figures from the International Monetary Fund show the nation's inflation is running lower than three of its ASEAN partners and its arch Asian export rivals, South Korea and Taiwan. Also the rise in consumer prices is slower than the average of the industrialised nations."

It went on to say: "but inflationary pressures levelled off because of the setting up of the National Wages Council, establishment of Welcome supermarket and the government build-up of rice stockpile" (see Appendix II).

I was a board member of Intraco back then, which was tasked by the government with the stockpiling of rice, as a security measure. This is because our main supply of rice was from Thailand. The Vietnam War had just extended into Cambodia and the fear was that our supplies could be cut off[3] should it spread further into Thailand. An official study at that time revealed that our stockpile would not last more than three months. So we tried securing alternative supply channels. The government wanted the country to have at least six months of supply, to be on the safe side. Intraco was given the task of managing the stockpile of not less than three months' worth. In addition, rice importers would be required to carry stocks of not less than three months' supply. NTUC Welcome took this opportunity to become one of the importers.

The Minister for Finance, Hon Sui Sen, sent a few of us to purchase rice from the United States. Now, rice cannot be kept for too long unless it is in *padi* form. So what we hoped to do was to stockpile *padi* in a series of large silos on the banks of the Mississippi River. The *padi* would be shipped to Singapore as and when required for further processing into rice. The leftover husks of the *padi* would be used to make animal and chicken feed meal. Given that importers would be obliged to have enough stocks to last three months, the country should manage quite well with the silos as emergency rations.

As I stated earlier, NTUC Welcome became a rice importer, moving into the territory of the big guys. One bad thing though, our success led many of our members of parliament to try to jump on the bandwagon. They set up consumer clubs to sell essential items like rice and sugar, to show they cared for the old and the poor. Kim San had to defend me in Parliament against accusations that Welcome was trying to create a cartel.[4] These came from the MP for Whampoa, Dr Augustine Tan, who claimed in Parliament that Welcome was pressurizing these clubs to raise the price of rice. I asked for him to repeat his accusation outside of Parliament, but he replied that he only had circumstantial evidence. He then went further to hint that Intraco was selling rice at a cheaper price to Welcome. Kim San continued defending me publicly, but after discussions, I decided to go public myself to defend Welcome and to explain how Augustine Tan's claims could not be true.[5] Quite frankly, the rice business was not a profitable one for Welcome in those days, although most people thought so.

Over the years Welcome worked very hard to start up as many outlets as possible as well as FairPrice shops. By the end of 1977, there were about 10 supermarkets and 160 FairPrice shops in Singapore.[6]

I announced to the press in January 1979 that Welcome had come of age. It was not even six years old yet and, discounting the role we played in combating inflation, we were making a profit of $271,862 from a total sale of $40 million. This was only 0.68 per cent of sales; we were not exactly a profit-maximizing outfit.

I was very proud of Welcome's many achievements, but in the end, I had to leave.[7] This was on 1 July 1982, nine years after I joined. The journalist Irene Ngo interviewed me then, and I remember telling her: "Nothing has been as close to me as Welcome. Every time I talk about Welcome, I feel a lump in my throat. But there comes a time when you have to go and let somebody take over."[8]

When Goh Chok Tong left NTUC Income in 1981, Dr Goh Keng Swee, who was now Deputy Prime Minister, wanted me to take over Income as well. I declined and from what I heard, this angered him greatly. There was always something Machiavellian and unforgiving about Dr Goh. But I was doing things for free, so when I did not feel like taking on something, I wouldn't.

Kim San and I were very close, and we often conversed in Hokkien to each other. So when I heard he was leaving as chairman of NTUC's board of trustees, I told him that I would also be leaving. A Hong Kong chain heard that I was resigning and approached me to work for them, to establish outlets here in Singapore for them. I said no, of course. I had been building up Welcome free of charge, doing it as a national service, fighting inflation. So it was a bit ridiculous of them to think that I would help them set up a competitor to Welcome.

Anyway, considering the fact that Welcome was not meant to be a profit-maximizing outfit, we did rather well. We kept inflation down, and if you look at our books, Welcome's net assets, valued at $864,428 in June 1974, had increased to $2,846,018 by June 1982.[9] More than that, we kept our books in such detail that we were never in trouble economically. We monitored every detail. I didn't take chances. We would even vary our use of our decentralized air-conditioning system according to the time of day and the crowd.

INTERNATIONAL TRADING COMPANY (INTRACO) (1969–1986)

I mentioned earlier that I was involved in the International Trading Company (Intraco) — a founding director, in fact. It was started by Dr Goh Keng Swee, and the first chairman was Hon Sui Sen, who at that time was not a Minister yet. He was then chairman of the Economic Development Board (EDB).

I stayed at Intraco for seventeen long years, and sad to say, when I left, it was under less than happy circumstances. In fact,

I resigned in protest against a decision being taken by the rest of the board against my objections. I just could not stay after that. On principle, I just could not continue. So I resigned on 29 April 1986. Chandra Das, who was managing director, resigned around the same time for other reasons.

What happened was this. A big Indonesian businessman had bought 15 per cent of the company and wished to have a seat on the board. He was to be represented there by Lee Kim Yew from the Singapore law firm, Lee & Lee. The board had in principle agreed to this.

At that time, it consisted of, among others, representatives from DBS, EDB, Sheng-Li Holdings with Lien Ying Chow as the Chairman and Ngiam Tong Dow as the Deputy Chairman and Chairman of the executive committee.

What I wish to talk about was this important meeting from which I stormed out. The papers for this 58th Board meeting on 29 April 1986 had been sent out about ten days or so earlier. And as usual, I had prepared for the meeting with the help of my group corporate accountant. But a day before the actual meeting, a notice came to say that there was a mistake and the papers were to be withdrawn and replaced by new ones. Not having time to involve others to help me go through the new papers, I spent the night doing it all by myself, jotting down points and questions. I came up with a list of seven queries which I then sent to the Company Secretary to be tabled at the meeting (see Appendix III).

Intraco was a very powerful company back then, having been entrusted with managing the rice stockpile and imports and exports from the Eastern bloc countries. It appeared that this Indonesian businessman was aiming to take over the company.

I was quite taken aback by the declaration in the newspapers that we were making a loss of about $500,000 instead of a profit. What was happening was that provisions were suddenly being made for losses for diminution in value of investment of $1.136 million, and $1.262 million by subsidiaries and $2.790 million in doubtful debts, amounting to a total of $5.188 million.

We were about to make public a report with a loss of $500,000, and at a time when someone out there was aggressively buying our shares. Of course, I protested, but the board was largely against me, saying that I was splitting hairs and that these were just provisions and not real losses. I said that was exactly the reason I could not agree to it. Once this went out, Intraco shares would drop, and at a time when someone was looking to buy into the company. My objections were duly noted but the report was to be adopted anyway. I threatened to walk out if they passed it. And when they did exactly that, I stormed out. I then called up First Deputy Prime Minister Goh Chok Tong to tell him about it and to ask him to take action. On resigning, I had to answer questions from the press, and we decided that I would say that seventeen years on the board was enough for me, and that it was time to leave. First DPM Goh told me to write to the Chairman of Temasek Holdings (Pte) Ltd with a copy to him and promised me that he would act on the matter. This he did the following year, when the board was changed.[10]

What followed confirmed my suspicion. An offer by Morgan Grenfell (Asia) Limited on behalf of United Industrial Corporation Limited (UIC) to acquire all the issued ordinary shares of $1.00 each fully paid in the capital of Intraco Limited, other than those already owned by UIC, was subsequently made on 26 June 1986 (see Appendix IV).

SINGAPORE CORPORATION OF REHABILITATIVE ENTERPRISES (SCORE) (1975–1987)

The Singapore Corporation of Rehabilitative Enterprises (SCORE) was established on 7 November 1975 through the Singapore

Corporation of Rehabilitative Enterprises Act 1975. It is a statutory board created to bring about the rehabilitation of prisoners. In doing so, SCORE assumed the tasks of the former Prison Industries, whose operations it officially took over in April 1976. SCORE administered the rehabilitative programmes for Changi Prison, the Medium Security Prison, the Queenstown Remand Prison, the Reformative Training Centre, a section of Moon Crescent Centre, the Female Prison and Chia Keng Prison. Rehabilitation was to be achieved through the inculcation of work discipline. In 1977, it widened its responsibility to include the Drug Rehabilitation Centres (DRCs).

From the start, I was very much involved in it and decided to take on the task as general manager as well. I must say that I am very proud of what I accomplished during my twelve years as chairman of SCORE. The ten years working under Chua Sian Chin, the Minister for Home Affairs, was a real pleasure. I had immediate access to him and we managed to get things done very quickly.

SCORE was very personal to me because I believe it required a lot of me as a person to see it through, relying on my insights on humanity, my understanding of what it is like to be down and out, my sense of what is practicable and what is not, and my sense of business. I had to mobilise my whole being to make SCORE succeed. In fact, it was due to SCORE that some of the successes we had with the Singapore Anti-Narcotics Association (SANA) were possible. It was with SCORE's help that enough accommodation could be arranged in a very short time for the huge numbers of drug addicts detained under Operation Ferret. But let's talk about SANA and Operation Ferret later.

Before SCORE, we had something called Prison Industries, a department under the Prisons. It was spending a lot of money and was producing things such as furniture which was unsellable. They had warehouse after warehouse of the unwanted stuff. After an inquiry, Devan Nair rightly decided that a statutory board should be formed to take over from them. The major concern for the succeeding organization was that the financials must be clearly accounted for. I was called up by Chua Sian Chin, the Minister for Home Affairs, and asked to become the chairman. I accepted. I recalled telling the then head of civil service, George Bogaars, of my appointment and his reply was, "Good Lord, you are chairman of SCORE? That is dead even before it is born."

When we started SCORE in 1975, we were promised a $5 million capital grant and an annual grant of $218,000. This may sound very strange today, but I declined to draw on these grants, feeling confident that we would manage without the money. We did manage. When I left twelve years later, SCORE had a surplus of $24 million, with functioning innovations brought in by me such as solar panels for energy supply and reconditioned laundry equipment that proved to be extremely efficient. It was a growing concern when I left.

You see, the money was for us to buy new laundry machines and to subsidize the projected loss. I decided that we could recondition and upgrade the old machines that we had in storage. They were mostly heavy machinery made of cast iron using conveying belts. We were able to replace the conveying belt with gears. Once I had decided to do that, I made sure the Ministry was informed.

I was offered an office in Prison Headquarters, and I remember my wife Daisy telling me that she did not want to have to tell friends that I went to prison every morning. Anyway, we set up office at the Singapore National Stadium, and the good thing about that was that we got to watch football matches for free. Also, there were squash courts close by. So I took up the sport, and Stephen Goh, the secretary, and I would play a game or two every other day before showering for work. Otherwise, I would jog a bit. Even after I stopped working at SCORE, I continued to drop by to play squash with Stephen. I continued with the sport after I moved to Germany.

Prison rehabilitation was in a shambles when SCORE started. According to the prison director, inmate fighting was a big problem, especially in what was called the Reformative Training Centre (RTC). The prisoners were under 21 years of age and something like 30 per cent of them were involved in fights among themselves.

Within six months, we had created over a thousand new jobs, and once our prisoners were earning money, the fighting stopped. We even had an electronic assembly factory in the RTC. By the end of 1976, we had 89 per cent of our 4,000 prisoners employed profitably, compared to 45.5 per cent before SCORE came into being.

The private sector was encouraged to offer jobs to prisoners, and by early 1977, four companies had agreed to participate. These were Industrial Electronics and Engineering, Singapore Woodcraft Manufacturing, Shimano, and Seasonal Garment Manufacturing. Payment for the labour went to SCORE, and after deductions for overhead expenses, prisoners received between $2.40 and $6.80 daily, depending on their skill level. The industries operated by SCORE were laundry and bakery. We went into furniture and printing operations later. By 1984, apart from our own production, we had nine private companies operating fourteen factories in various penal institutions under this Private Participation Scheme to prepare inmates for their release.

We exported rattan cane furniture and some other products to Australia. Complaints cropped up, however, and our customer said they couldn't buy from us because we were using prison labour and exploiting the prisoners. I told them to visit us to study what we were doing before they formed an opinion. They actually came, and after that, they allowed the imports. Amnesty International also got into the act of criticizing us. Chua Sian

Chin called me up and told me to ignore them. But seriously, our prisoners were being treated better than anywhere else. They worked and they helped support their families. What more could they want?

We introduced a training scheme at the RTC where inmates worked a full eight-hour-day producing digital clocks for the American and European markets. Certificates of competency from the Vocational and Industrial Training Board were handed out to those who passed, and a majority of them did pass.

A compulsory savings scheme was also set up for the inmates with the Post Office Savings Bank, with their dependants being given the right to draw on these accounts even while their sentence was being served.[11] The Director of Prisons, Quek Shi Lei, who was the CEO at SCORE arranged for 40 per cent of their earnings to go into such accounts, while the rest of their earnings could be used for purchases at the Welcome co-operative supermarkets that were set up there.

To exemplify what the problems were, and how we had to innovate to improve matters, let me tell you this story. The first time I visited the laundry facility run by Prisons Industries, I saw that a lot of things were not right. I went back a few times, bringing along my technicians from my company for advice. I had taken a look in the books and saw that the water and energy bills added up annually to $1.5 million! What a shock that was. That was why I brought in some innovations, such as solar panels. The solar panels could heat up the water to 20°C at best and the boilers would then boost the water temperature to the required 45°C. We actually managed to cut electricity costs by half. Where water use was concerned, the problem was that most of the dirty linen came from hospitals. These were of course badly soiled with blood and other nasty things. So it was a dirty and smelly job separating the sheets from human excreta and even body parts, not to mention the volumes of blood soaked into the textile.

To keep them clean and free of bacteria, the laundry was subjected to five rinses, and the last rinse was with the water heated up in boilers up to 45°C to kill the bacteria. That was why the recurrent cost of energy and water was $1.5 million a year.

I came up with the idea to reuse water from the second rinse in the third rinse, and do the same with last two rinses. The first rinse was too awful to be reused. In that way, we saved two rinses. I brought in my own engineers, and together we added a pedal system to the washing machines which could direct water to flow the way we wanted into a series of drains leading to recycling and filtering pools. This took months and a lot of thinking to work out. Again, this is something I am very proud of. I don't know if people higher up knew what we accomplished. Chua Sian Chin certainly knew, since he did read my reports.

Cutting down on electricity use and water use alone saved us at least half a million dollars annually. We were already making a profit in the first year.

We began encouraging manufacturers to establish within our facilities. We offered lower rents, and we guaranteed them workers at 10 to 15 per cent cheaper wages. More importantly, we guaranteed them that the number of workers would be constant. We would replace any sick workers immediately. That way, their costs of production were guaranteed to go down.

Even pianos were being made in the prisons at that time. That was how we managed to finance everything we did. As I said, the year I left, we had a $24 million surplus. Things were working very well. We had foreign visitors coming to study us. For example, W. Clifford, the Director of the Australian Institute of Criminology, was taken for a study tour of SCORE's work in January 1978 (see Appendix V).

I also had an idea when I learned that prisoners were being released after serving two-thirds of their sentence for good behaviour. In fact this was done automatically. A paper was drawn up and presented to the ministry. In it, SCORE offered to help the released inmates set up companies and secure orders for them in the skills they were trained in, such as barbering, electrical and engineering work, if, instead of being released for good behaviour, they could be attached to SCORE during the last one third of their time. Chua took it to the prime minister, which was Lee Kuan Yew at that time, and I was subsequently told that although he liked the idea, it could not work for constitutional reasons. It impinged into the area of the Judiciary. He was right of course.

If SCORE had been allowed to help them start up enterprises that were in time handed over to them, we could have done a lot of good rehabilitating these prisoners. We had the money to do this, and this money had come from the prisoners anyway. More importantly it would be much easier for SCORE than for the prisoners to get orders from say the Public Works Department, Housing & Development Board and private companies. Had I stayed on longer at SCORE, I might have looked into how we could have solved the problem through some innovation. But that was not to be. That was one of the things I regret not doing. I could have discussed the matter further with Wee Chong Jin, the Chief Justice, for example. But I didn't.

On a personal note, I was able to work with Ministers such as Dr Toh Chin Chye, Lim Kim San or Chua Sian Chin, and to have good rapport with them. We treated each other as equals. But Chua left already on 1 January 1985. The new Minister for Home Affairs was S. Jayakumar. Feeling that I had done enough,

I decided to leave my various commitments, giving him time to find replacements for me. All in all, I worked twelve years at SCORE, ten years under Chua, and two under Jayakumar.

It was common knowledge in those days that Prison Industries was a disaster, and that it was SCORE that turned things around.[12]

COMMITTEE ON TREATMENT AND REHABILITATION OF DRUG ADDICTS (1977–1988) AND SINGAPORE ANTI-NARCOTICS ASSOCIATION (SANA) (1977–1996)

In the 1970s, the treatment of drug addicts by any private organization, including private doctors, was forbidden by law. The rationale was that addicts are desperate people and are therefore easily exploited by those supposedly treating them. As we know, when an addict is looking for his next dose, he will do anything.

In those early days, I dare say that there were no experts in the world on the epidemic drug problem. The plague of drug abuse hit everyone unexpectedly. The Americans were the ones who started using methadone as replacement for heroin. Now, heroin destroys your liver, and other internal organs, resulting in death. It is a tolerance drug which requires the addict to take heavier doses just to get the same euphoria. The same dosage will not help. Methadone is not such a drug, but it is addictive nevertheless. It was realized that methadone is more addictive than heroin, and that addiction to methadone can lead to death as well.

Now, there were three ways of treating heavily addicted persons. One was the use of replacement drugs; the second, the "cold turkey" method; and the third was through reduced dosage. The last was not an effective method. So, Singapore decided to go for the cold turkey method. Addicts were put in a special room and they went through the pangs of withdrawal under constant watch. They suffered nausea, diarrhoea and all kinds of pain. They went through this for a few days. After that, they would be totally worn out, and we made sure that they were properly fed and then nursed back to health.

While other countries resorted to methadone, Singapore did not. Methadone was popular partly because you do not see the suffering. Weaning the users off that drug was not an easy thing and many died. We had a small population and valued every person, so that was the main reason we decided on the cold turkey method. Since most of our addicts were not seriously addicted, this method worked quite smoothly. Most of the addicts inhaled, and only a handful injected heroin. I wouldn't recommend the same treatment where addiction is widespread and serious. For our serious cases, and these were narrowed down to only a few, personal attention was given them by our doctors. We had to be very careful with these addicts.

I know a lot about this because I was in the thick of constructing and conceptualizing the solution to the problem. I was helping drug addicts for over twenty years, through the Singapore Anti-Narcotics Association (SANA). When we started, we were as ignorant as anyone else. And the situation was epidemic in scale, hitting alarming figures within a few years. The Government had to act fast and effectively.

Something called the Committee on Treatment and Rehabilitation of Drug Addicts was set up under Chua Sian Chin, the Minister for Health and Home Affairs, on 9 February 1977. At the time, I was already chairman of the Metrication Board, NTUC Welcome and SCORE. But I was asked to chair this new committee anyway. I suspect this had something to do with me returning the grant that they gave me to run SCORE. The fact that I was from the private sector was also a consideration they had.

My work in the other boards meant that I already knew most of the ministers and members of parliament. After my appointment, I would be called up often to Chua's office for discussions about the drug problem. This would be at 9 am in the morning, and I would be the first visitor. After a couple of visits, I couldn't understand why I had to wait at least 10 minutes outside the door before he would see me. I didn't feel too comfortable or happy about that. This must have been obvious to his personal assistant who then told me the reason why I had to wait. Chua wanted to serve me coffee hot. She was instructed to switch on the kettle when I arrived to make the pot of coffee and only after that, was I to be ushered into the room. I then realized that each time I came into his room, Chua was always holding up the coffee pot to pour coffee for me.

How do you say no to a man like that? He was extremely humble, and we became very close friends. I would do anything for him. I mean, I was working for free anyway. If I did not like something, it did not matter if you paid me a million dollars, I wouldn't have taken it on anyway. But Chua — like Lee Kuan Yew — was someone who could reach out to you, touch you, touch your feelings. Although we sometimes had loud and heated arguments, we always ended up as friends. We had strong mutual respect for each other.

Despite my initial doubts about the job, I went around at the time finding out from various concerned authorities about the issues involved in addict detention, drug rehabilitation, and such matters. I even went to see Dr Toh Chin Chye about my doubts, and how Chua would not take no for an answer. But after resisting pressure from Chua for three months, I finally accepted the job. I did tell him my family's worries. My wife and children feared that drug traffickers would target me and my family. Chua offered me a bodyguard, and I said that would only make it worse. So, he offered me a pistol. And for a long time, I actually did carry a gun on me. I even went for some training in how to handle a gun. But whatever the circumstances, when you are in possession of something like that, you become very self-conscious of it and of the dangers you are living under.

Now, the normal administrative process for handling drug addict cases would not have worked. The plague was spreading too quickly. From the start, we made sure that the committee consisted of all the directors of the ministries involved. That way, any decision we made would go straight back to the ministries, to the permanent secretaries, and be carried out immediately. We needed to work that fast. No bureaucracy at all. That was how the Misuse of Drugs Act (1973) introduced by Chua in Parliament in 1972 was passed so quickly.

As chairman of the Committee on the Treatment and Rehabilitation of Drug Addicts, I had immediate contact with a group of permanent secretaries. However, the infrastructure for my work was far from sufficient. After immersing myself in the drug problem for about three months, I went to see Chua. The committee needed more help if we were to succeed. We had to have some public association to care for the addicts. We needed more volunteers. So Chua mentioned the possibility of me taking over SANA, which at that time had quite a bad reputation. There had been allegations of exploitation of addicts and even funds going missing.

I agreed to take over SANA on condition that I would be responsible only for things that happened after I came. Anything that went before would have nothing to do with me. To be sure, I don't know if this point was put into the records, and I don't know if those who took over after Chua knew anything about this limit on the responsibility I was demanding, or about what we later achieved at SANA. If not, then some serious misunderstanding about my role might have taken place after Chua left.

Tellingly, when we had a meeting to formalize my chairmanship of SANA, none of the members of the old board turned up except for the president, Tow Siang Hwa. They had resigned en bloc. So I had to quickly call K.S. Rajah for help. He came, and we took over SANA. I was president and he was vice-president. Later, I had to bring over my own people from the Metrication Board, from SCORE and from NTUC Welcome to fill the board. That was the only thing I could do.

We had to rewrite SANA's constitution. The three people responsible for SANA's success, I would say today were K.S. Rajah, who was director of the legal aid bureau, K.V. Veloo who was our Chief Probation and Aftercare Officer, and me. Veloo set up the new SANA Aftercare Counselling Services and became its secretary. Matters dealing with the law were handled by K.S. Rajah. Being a businessman, management matters were not a problem for me. So, between the three of us, we got SANA going, and I was working sixteen hours a day.

In fact, it was K.S. Rajah who brought my attention to the constitutional restriction against long-term detention. No one was allowed to be held for more than twenty-four hours without being brought before a judge. So I went to Chua Sian Chin, who took the matter to the Cabinet and we actually changed that law to exclude drug addicts for the time being. We also made sure that the detainees would not be stigmatized either. The Central Narcotics Bureau (CNB) would keep track of them but the Criminal Record Office would not have any record of these people in their files.

But just as important was the relationship we had to have with other government authorities involved in this new work that we were taking on. We would have to have intimate dealings with the police and the prisons, for example. Again, I was lucky on that point. The chief executive officer at SCORE was the Director of Prisons, Quek Shi Lei. Because of the positions I was holding, things could come together smoothly.

Once I was in, Chua Sian Chin informed me that Operation Ferret was to be launched within a fortnight, and I had therefore to put together a treatment programme as soon as possible. This was in mid-March 1977. An estimated 15,000 persons were to be detained. The basic idea was to separate the hard-core drug addicts from those who were not yet addicted. However, one could not detain these people without having a credible treatment and rehabilitation programme to present to the general public and to the parents of these boys and girls. I stared at him incredulously. How were we to come up with such a treatment programme in so short a time? No such programme existed in the world then. So, I got my board together to try to figure something out.

This was when what I can only describe as a miracle took place. I couldn't sleep for nights on end after that. But about a week later, I suddenly woke up in the middle of the night, at 3 o'clock. I had a vision just before waking up of the entire programme in my head. I quickly grabbed a pen and paper, and jotted down everything I could. The next morning, I handed my notes to be typed out by my secretary at SCORE. That programme then went smoothly through the committee, the minister and then the Cabinet.

Believe it or not, this programme has not been fundamentally changed since then. There is only the addition of a further stage after the release of the addicts. Otherwise, the programme was close to perfect. I still do not quite understand how I managed that, scribbling away in the middle of the night, and coming up with a programme in two hours. I have since spoken all over the world about the stages involved.

I suppose the three months when I walked around talking to people who were working on the drug problem helped my mind to think deeply about things. But waking up in the middle of the night with the solution... some Invisible Hand must have helped me. I am really not that smart.

Basically, the rehabilitation programme was designed for a six-month stay at the centre. But those who relapsed repeatedly could, through a later amendment in the Misuse of Drugs Act, be kept at the centre for up to three years.[13]

- Stage One: Seven days of mandatory detoxification by cold turkey. Medication is only given in a life-threatening situation, and inmates aged 55 or more are exempted;
- Stage Two: One week for recuperation and reorientation conducted by the staff;
- Stage Three: One week of intensive sessions by a doctor, a psychologist and social service officers to drive home the evils of the drug habit, the realities of life and the meaningful part the inmate can play in society;
- Stage Four: From the fourth week to the end of the third month, a military form of training to inculcate discipline and promote physical wellness is implemented; starting with light calisthenics to obstacle courses and jogging. In this stage, inmates take part in daily flag raising ceremonies, kit inspections and general cleaning chores;
- Stage Five: During the last three months, inmates are put in workshops for eight hours a day and earn standard wages plus other activities to prepare them for employment.

On 1 April 1977, a countrywide round-up of addicts by the whole police force and the central narcotics bureau was actually carried out, leading to about 13,000 persons being put into detention centres. During the whole of Operation Ferret, as many as

800 persons per month were being detained. Unfortunately, the Malays were strongly over-represented among the addicts, easily making up three-quarters of the detainees. The drug epidemic began in the Malay community, and exploded from there. A lot of peer influence I believe.

The committee, which was me, had to supply the accommodation for these people. Costs threatened to be prohibitive. Luckily, I was chairman of SCORE as well. Now, the British military withdrawal had left the many bungalows at Seletar Airbase empty, and these were under the jurisdiction of the Ministry of Finance. And so, Veloo and I went to see the Finance Minister.

We were allowed to take charge of the buildings in the airbase. The bungalows had three rooms each, and we managed to convert each house to accommodate as many as 50 detainees. We also had to put up steel bars on all the windows and to reinforce the ceiling before they could be used for proper detention of the addicts. So we actually got prisoners to do that for us. The man who was placed in charge of construction at SCORE was a prison superintendent called Anthony Gloss. He managed to convert 200 places ready for me within a week ahead of the detention. He was a very capable man.

There was a problem that at first seemed insurmountable. This was the painful lack of toilets. The bungalows were originally built to take five occupants, not fifty. Fortunately, I was at the same time a member of the HDB, and I remembered that it was building a lot of one-room flats at that time, and of course they had bought a lot of toilets for this.

We went to Teh Cheang Wan. He was not Minister for National Development yet. At that time, he was the Chief Executive Officer of the HDB. I asked for the toilets to be used for the drug programme, and he kindly agreed to it. We soon had enough toilets for the detainees, lined up in rows and connected to the nearby sewage systems. From that point on, we just kept doubling our manpower when accommodation was needed. Drug rehabilitation centres were set up all over the country, and we managed to match the speed of the detention of addicts.

My first year as SANA president was a most exciting though difficult one. The Minister left it all to me. We had nothing to start with, no infrastructure that was suitable; nothing like that. We were in need of funds as well. So I went to Dr Toh Chin Chye, who called up Hon Sui Sen, and everything was basically fixed from then on. George Edwin Bogaars was the Permanent Secretary at the Ministry of Finance then. I remember a civil servant asking me a lot of questions when I was there, but Bogaars cut him off and told him not to ask so much and anyway, the minister had already said to give me the money.

In a rehabilitation programme, a lot of volunteers are needed. I saw this most clearly in the halfway houses, where volunteers were recruited to help with counselling and aftercare. Now, given the scale of the problem following Operation Ferret, how were we to handle things? We were dealing with people of varied cultural backgrounds. Those arrested when Operation Ferret first started in April 1977 were due to be released in September that year. To prepare for that, we formed the Aftercare Coordinating Committee whose job it was to solve the acute shortage of counsellors needed for drug addicts on their release.

Again, the answer came to me in the middle of the night. I woke up with one word in my head: Religion! Next morning, I got my secretary to call up all the leaders of the major religions in Singapore to come for a meeting: the Mufti, the abbot, Archbishop Gregory Yong, you name it. So they all came. I remember the occasion very well. I entered the meeting hall adjacent to my office and said, "Good morning, ladies and gentlemen, the government needs your help and you cannot refuse". I could see that they were shocked by my statement. I then added "We need your help to save lives; to save lives in your own flock." Well, of course they couldn't refuse.

By late August, eleven religious groups had come on board.[14] Within one year, I had 1,000 volunteers from among them. The problem remained only partially solved, however, and quite a number of former drug addicts remained without volunteer aftercare officers.

The official figure for Muslim addicts without aftercare officers was very high — 79.7 per cent in December 1978.[15] You see, drug addiction spreads socially. I think in the case of Singapore, the habit started among Malays, and so it spread most rapidly in that community. A Muslim leader told me that even six months or eight months after Operation Ferret, the Muslim counsellors were still being visited by these addicts. They were often lonely people and appreciated talking to their religious leaders. Many became more religious. You know, we gave the detainees crew cuts when they were taken in, and we gave them crew cuts when they left. So, one could see short-haired boys queuing up outside the mosques quite often.

At first, the mosques would not allow any activity other than the preaching of the Koran. So we had to discuss matters with Muslim members of parliament. They were very helpful. I spoke to the civil service as well, and they talked to the Mufti. Finally, they changed the regulations, and decided to allow speeches on the drug problem in adjacent buildings, though not in the mosque itself. That made a lot of difference.

Another problem was that of narco-dogs at the Causeway customs checkpoint. These animals had to climb into cars to sniff for drugs, and would sometimes salivate on the seats. As you can imagine, there were a lot of complaints about this. So, we had to get the help of the Mufti again, who talked to the Mufti on the Malaysian side. They decided that the dog's saliva was not *haram*, and that one needed merely to wash off the saliva. The Koran itself apparently never mentions dogs being *haram*. That was another achievement for us.

The Christians were very enthusiastic from the start. Soon after I was appointed chairman of the Committee on the Treatment and Rehabilitation of Drug Addicts, the first director of Central Narcotics Bureau, John Hanam, brought me to a number of halfway houses. They had groups of young boys and girls singing hymns, saying Jesus had saved them. Being an eternal sceptic, I told John Hanam to pick them up and test their urine. True enough, two out of the four were still on drugs. One thing I have learned is that drug addicts are amazing liars. They can lie to you right to your face and you wouldn't be able to tell. The only way to know for sure is to test them. I told the pastor the problem: he was doing a disservice by having in their drug prevention programme drug addicts who were claiming that they were cured.

I first met with Rev. Irvin Rutherford in 1977 soon after I was appointed chairman of the drug committee. He was the head of Teen Challenge halfway house then, and he told me their rehabilitation programme included the provision of treatment for drug addicts. I advised him against it. Initially, he was rather reluctant but subsequently he did agree to work closely with SANA to provide volunteer aftercare officers under SANA's Christian Counselling Services. Other religious groups began to set up their own counselling services. The Catholic Aftercare Counselling Services was set up followed by others formed by the Muslims, Hindus and the Buddhists, and even a number of secular groups such as the People's Association youth aftercare counselling services.

The various religions worked closely to take care of their own flocks and when their volunteers were insufficient, the addicts would be provided aftercare counselling services by volunteers from the secular groups.

On 14 May 1978, a columnist for the *Sunday Times*, Dr Nalla Tan, wrote an article claiming that the conditions in the DRCs were appalling. She had based her facts, according to her, on people who had been through the rehabilitation centres. She wrote about how the detainees had fleas in their hair, and how they had to defecate in pots in crowded cubicles. She said she had more to reveal the following Sunday. The article created an uproar and I was inundated with calls from members of parliament.

The Ministry of Home Affairs and SANA refuted the charges and threw open the DRCs for visits by the MPs. After the visits by the MPs and members of the news media, it was found that the charges were untrue and Dr Nalla Tan wrote a retraction the following week.

SANA also started an anti-drug abuse badge award scheme for school uniformed groups, such as the boy scouts, cadet corps and others. This award scheme was divided into two parts. In the first part, the boy would be tested for his knowledge on the dangers of drug abuse and in the second, he was asked for the names of the ten other boys that he had transferred his knowledge to. Only after the ten boys were tested and found to know about the dangers of drug abuse was the medal awarded. You see here that when a boy scout was awarded an anti-drug abuse badge, there would be another ten boys immunized against drug abuse. This was a self-generating aware scheme.

Through the Ministry of Home Affairs I was invited by the U.S. Embassy to visit the United States to study the treatment and rehabilitation programmes available there. I visited a number of privately run treatment centres. At the State Department,

I had to answer a lot of questions concerning treatment programme in Singapore. I was surprised by the numerous questions they put to me. I told them that I came to learn the U.S. drug treatment and rehabilitation system but instead they were asking about ours. It was then that they told me the actual situation.

One of them said: "Mr Baey, I will be honest with you. The Malaysian government approached us, asking for a treatment programme for their drug addicts. They are having enormous problems. We hear that you guys have been very successful with your programme, and since your cultures are similar, we thought we should learn from you and pass on that information to them."

That was a strange situation for me, as you can imagine. I was flabbergasted. The Malaysians could have come to us anytime for information if they had wanted to. But they didn't. They went to the Americans instead.

The main drugs of abuse were heroin and morphine. Later on, synthetic drugs also appeared. Marijuana was also a problem despite what many say about it being harmless. It is not. It is a dangerous drug. Research conducted by the University of Texas found that marijuana contained more than 280 types of chemicals and one of which, when smoked, would attach itself to the IQ part of the brain and make the person lethargic. Further studies revealed that it took about three months for the body to completely cleanse away that chemical. So if one were to smoke marijuana once a week, the natural process in the brain would not be able to clean it. Moreover, marijuana is known as a gateway drug because it tends to lead to the use of heavier drugs, such as morphine and heroin. Cocaine was not a serious problem for us then. It was more an upper class drug.

I also remember being invited to speak at a conference organized by the European Economic Community to discuss drug laws. They were in the process of drawing up such laws and wanted to hear from two experts — one with a tough drug programme, which was Singapore, in their eyes anyway, and the other was Sweden, which had a lenient approach to drug addiction. There were demonstrators outside with placards claiming Singapore hanged drug addicts, which was a strange allegation. I had to be smuggled in through the back door.

Anyway, I made it clear to the audience that Singapore did not hang addicts. On the contrary, we were spending an average of S$30,000 on each addict to treat and rehabilitate them. There were endless misconceptions among the participants and among the audience in general. One even asked, "Mr Baey, how many drug addicts have you people murdered?"

I had to inform him that he was perhaps referring to drug dealers. Visitors coming into Singapore were and are told the penalty for drug trafficking, which is the mandatory death sentence. I told them we hanged traffickers because they were the purveyors of death, they sold death.

Nevertheless, it was a measure of our success that the Americans and the Europeans would come to us to ask us for advice on the management of drug addiction. Our drug addict population did go down. Once in a while, someone would come up to me to say that he was a drug addict but was now running a transport company, or something like that. That gives me great satisfaction. I feel proud then.

Once we had a video conference at the East-West Center in Hawaii. I was the last to speak to Dr Dogoloff ,the drug advisor to President Carter, on the screen. I took them to task for giving grants to organizations to treat drug addicts, and basing these grants on their success rate. I argued that this simply meant that organizations would concentrate on those who were not seriously addicted in order to show good results and thus get better grants. My question then was, what happened to those who were really sick? That left them dumbstruck. They couldn't answer that one, except to say that it was the policy of the past administration.

Anyway, I was appreciated enough in the United States for the American Narcotics Enforcement Officers' Association of America to give me an International Award of Honour.

Now, back to SANA. The government's grant for SANA was only $99,000 a year, but we were spending $1.5 million annually. So I actually had to raise $1.4 million myself. Every year for twenty years, mind you. The work I did for SANA was quite incredible, when I think of it now. This was a big sum of money, and I had to make use of all my contacts in the business world to put together that amount. Aside from the foundations and others, there were two people I depended on. These were attached to the Goddess of Mercy Temple, the Guanyin Temple, on Waterloo Street; and the Kong Meng San Temple on Bright Hill Road. The chairman of the management committee of the Guanyin Temple, Yeo Tiam Siew, was a good friend of mine. They were very rich then, and he agreed to make up the difference every year. The Abbot of the Kong Meng San Monastery, Seck Hong Choon, was also very supportive.

I didn't believe in the method of raising money where whoever helped us got a cut and we kept the rest. I believed that whatever we collected had to go to the charity, except perhaps with a deduction for expenses. Exploitation came in too easily if you used the other method. We recorded everything, even donations of $10, and the annual report was circulated for all to see. This transparency helped us get even more support, I believe. My business connections came in very useful, there was a lot of goodwill. I can tell you that people in the metal business helped out a lot as well.

SANA had about 100 members paying $10 annually in fees, or $100 for life membership. Every two years, we held elections. Our clubhouse was at Scotts Road, and we moved later to what is now Eton School. I remember we had one-armed bandits placed there, and those actually generated enough for us to pay for operating costs at the club. These machines were bandits all right.

When I left in 1996, after twenty years as president, I was told that the government had finally decided to allocate an annual grant of $1.5 million to SANA. I was very happy about that, since that would make the organization's work so much easier.

For me, the drug committee and SANA's activities worked very well under Chua Sian Chin. Things got done because of our ability to act swiftly; and because we had direct access to a pro-active minister who understood what we were doing. If the committee had been only an advisory body, then things would have moved too slowly. Normal civil servants would not have dared to push some of the things we needed to have done.

There were times when I did not agree with Chua. Perhaps he had to consider instructions from other channels. In those cases, I would tell him that I did not agree with him, but I would do what he wanted anyway.

At the end of my term with SANA, I was asked to become administrator for the Kong Meng San Monastery. One day, the abbot came to me. He suspected that something was very wrong with the finances of the monastery, and he wanted me to look into it. So I went to the Minister, Jayakumar, to ask his advice. He warned me about the sensitivities concerning a religious organization, and that if I were to involve myself, it should be on a personal basis, and not as head of SANA or SCORE. I said alright. So I went in as administrator of the monastery for a year, and soon found out that top gangsters were involved in the finances of the monastery, and in running the crematorium. They recognized me as being the head of SCORE, and when I told them to relocate themselves since I was coming in as administrator, they actually did move out, and without causing even a ripple of trouble, believe it or not. We once caught people going through the collection boxes. I had a police officer with me then, and we arrested them. So I managed to clean all that up and put safety measures in place. I introduced new financial and management systems in Kong Meng San during the year I was with them. Anyway, we had stopped the leakage from the monastery, and it started to bloom. At this time, I was buying a big company in Germany and decided to leave. This meant resigning from the positions that I still held under the Ministry of Home Affairs. These would be the Drug Advisory Committee, SANA, and SCORE. Of those who had a hand in making SCORE a success, I was the only person not awarded a medal, although I was the one who started it up from scratch.

Under Chua, I took on all these jobs. Just as with my joining the HDB under Lim Kim San, I took on these positions because of friendship; because I could afford it after making loads of money in my Vietnam ventures; and because the country was not exactly rich in those days.

When I was about to leave SANA, I put in an application for a $1.5 million annual grant from the government. That was approved, which meant that my successors would not have to have the same trouble I had raising money endlessly. Anyway, for my work with SANA, I was awarded a BBM(L) by Wong Kan Seng, after he took over as Minister for Home Affairs. He had been reading my report.

In my experience working with these organizations, you must be able to give freely of your own heart. Nothing creative, nothing new, and nothing innovative will come out of it otherwise, and you will only be doing the state a disservice. You will not be able to inspire others to excel. As a private person who has been through the civil service system without being indebted to anyone, I can tell you this.

Now, my work with drug abuse also got me involved with the International Federation of Non-Government Organisation for the Prevention of Drug and Substance Abuse (IFNGO). This body was launched in 1981 by Malaysia's former Prime Minister, Dr Mahathir Mohamad, with Australia, Hong Kong, Indonesia, Malaysia, Nepal, the Philippines, Singapore, Sri Lanka and Thailand as members.[16] Singapore through SANA took on the responsibility of keeping the accounts, at least while I was in charge. It was during this time that I was called to Washington when the State Department picked my brains in order to put together a programme for the Malaysians, who had approached them for one. In any case, I was given an award by Malaysia for my work with drugs. Incidentally, Thailand's National Council on Social Welfare also honoured me with a Plaque of Honour.

In September 1990, I was conferred a Doctor of Science degree in Perth by the Open University for Complementary Medicines and Medicina Alternativa, and people have called me Dr Baey since then. I am still a roving ambassador for the IFNGO, covering East Europe. I helped the Soviet Union set up its anti-drug abuse programme. They had no money but I did what I could, winning an award in the process.

Summarily, our success was due to the fact that we did not allow treatment. Addicts are very vulnerable people, and unless you have impeccable people treating them, they are going to be exploited in all sorts of ways. That's why I believe in the cold turkey method. By that, we meant no replacement drug.

We seem to have moved away from that nowadays. I don't know who is responsible for that.

ST JOHN AMBULANCE (1991–1998)

The St John Ambulance movement is an international organization that came to Singapore already before the war — in

1935, to be more exact. By 1991, it had 8,000 members. Under the council are found the Singapore St John Ambulance Association, run by a director, and the Singapore St John Brigade, placed under a commissioner.

At the end of 1991, the newspapers made it known that I had been elected chairman of the National St John Council. There is an unknown story behind that. After all, I took over from Mrs Cecilia Wee, the wife of the Chief Justice, Wee Chong Jin.

The position came to me by default, basically. One evening in late 1991, I met Mrs Wee at a party. She told me that she was chairman of St John, and would like me to come with her to a board meeting. She needed my advice, she said. Well, I found it hard to say "No" to her, she being the CJ's wife and all that.

Now, when I turned up at the meeting, I saw that something was amiss. For one thing, there was a crowd waiting outside the room where the meeting was being held, including journalists. I went in, and could immediate feel the animosity between the board members and Mrs Wee. I learned on the side that a vote of no confidence was going to be taken against her.

She introduced me as being from SANA and other boards. What could not escape me was that these people were eminent doctors and physicians. Whether I was brought there to give moral support to Mrs Wee or not was not an issue with them. They couldn't care less who I was.

They sat quietly, saying nothing. Well, time went by and the reporters outside were waiting for news. So I felt I had to act. I advised Mrs Wee to go to her office and wait there for word from me while I had a discussion with the other board members. Mrs Wee agreed, but on condition that I chaired the meeting in her absence. I said alright, but I was really going to have a conversation with them, and there was no need for a chair. And she left.

I then said: "Gentlemen. I really do not know head from tail here. Can you tell me what's going on?"

Well, that's when everything came out. They were so unhappy with Mrs Wee that they had written to the Queen of England. St John is affiliated to the Order of St John in the United Kingdom, after all. They were at their wit's end and were willing to give up totally on the organization. I told them to calm down. There were reporters waiting outside, and we should resolve this problem quickly.

My solution to the impasse was for the board to promote her to become President of St John. She could represent the organization at all the important events, and one of the others could become the chairman and run things the way the board wanted.

They had nothing against that; all they wanted was to serve the sick and needy anyway. So that seemed settled. I had Mrs Wee called back, and proposed that she be promoted to president of the council. That way, she could leave the nitty-gritty matters to a new chairman chosen from among the others. After some thought, she said she would agree, but on one condition, and that was that I, Baey Lian Peck, should become the chairman.

I protested of course. I already had too much on my plate. But she was adamant: either me as chairman or no deal. By now, the doctors were also trying to convince me.

Finally, I had to give in. I said I would be chairman for a year, and during that time, I would not tolerate any interference from the president. To my surprise, she agreed, saying that she knew me and knew my track record, and so on and so forth.

Well, the first month, she actually did not interfere. But by the second month, she would call or show up, complaining about how things were not being done properly. Things got a bit unbearable. In the end, I had to tell her that she was the elected president of the council and I was the elected chairman. Should she continue interfering, then I as chairman would get the council to have her sacked.

"I dare you," she challenged me.

After a while, I did draft a letter sacking her. I told the council that I would bear whatever financial costs might come out of it. Sure enough, a letter came from her lawyer — her son, incidentally — within a week. But about three months later, he called me up, saying: "Uncle Baey, let's drop the matter. Let's put it behind us."

I was of course very happy to do that, and so that was the end of that.

Anyway, things went more smoothly at St John after that, and I stayed until 1998. I did contribute something substantial though. Mrs Wee had told me that the property on which St John stood, on which it still stands, was held on a Temporary Occupation Licence (TOL) and that she had managed to have the annual fee paid for twenty years. Now I was on the HDB, and I knew that a TOL could not be valid for that long. Something was not right. So I asked my manager to check it out at the archives, and to get back to me with information on what the situation actually was. He found out that a lease on the land had been given to St John by the Commissioner of Lands, Mr Kwa Soon Chuan. This meant that we owned the land, and it was worth about $300 million at that time. So we set about getting a new title deed. This took much longer than I had expected. All the members from the early board of trustees had died, hence no one knew anything about the matter. That was why I left St John much later than I had planned.

Notes

1. The seven basic SI Units are metre (m) for length, kilogram (kg) for mass, second (s) for time, ampere (A) for electrical current, kelvin (K) for thermodynamic temperature, candela (cd) for luminous intensity and mole (mol) for amount of matter.

2. "Premier warns suppliers: Don't discriminate against WELCOME supermarket", *Straits Times*, 23 July 1973.

3. According to Intraco's official website, the company was incorporated on 5 November 1968. Its "original mission was to source competitively priced raw materials, commodities and manufactured goods to support Singapore's early industrialisation programme, which included the creation of new export markets for locally manufactured products, and the promotion of external trade". See <http://www.intraco.com.sg/>.

4. See "Intraco is not supplying rice at a cheaper price to Welcome: Baey", *New Nation*, 17 January 1979; and "Welcome says it again: Dr Tan's charge not true", *Straits Times*, 18 January 1979.

5. See "Intraco is not supplying rice at a cheaper price to Welcome: Baey", *New Nation*, 17 January 1979.

6. The inflation rate for Singapore in the first seven months of 1978 was 5.3%. Although this was higher than comparable periods over the last three years, it was lower than in countries such as the Philippines (7.2%), Thailand (9.1%), Indonesia (11%), Taiwan (8%), and South Korea (12.4%). The inflation average for industrialized countries for this period was 6.4%. "Singapore checks inflation's rise", *Straits Times*, 11 September 1978 (see Appendix II).

7. See Appendix VIII, which is a letter written by Baey to Prime Minister Lee Hsien Loong about how cross-subsidization can continue to be useful.

8. "Baey bids farewell to Welcome", *Straits Times*, 11 May 1982.

9. See Welcome Annual Reports for 1974 and 1982.

10. See "Men at the helm", *Straits Times*, 30 June 1978; "Intraco changes", in "Intraco appoints three new directors", *Straits Times*, 10 April

1987. It is reported that Intraco, which was first listed in 1972 made its first ever loss in 1985 of $1.3 million, and rebounded strongly into the black in 1986, making a profit of $6.3 million. See also *Straits Times*, 22 May 1986, where it is reported that in 1986, Baey Lian Peck, Teo Soo Chuan the industrialist, and Chandra Das resigned from the board while Tan Soo Nan and Lee Kim Yew joined.

11. See "Scoring 1,100 more jobs for prisoners", *Sunday Times*, October 1976; "The Govt organizes an 'inside job'", *Business Times*, 18 February 1977; "Factory extraordinary...where all workers are prisoners", *New Nation*, 25 May 1977; and "A Score of success", *Straits Times*, 15 February 1978.

12. For a clearer picture of what SCORE was about, and how it was run, see Appendix VI, a speech made by Baey Lian Peck at a SCORE dinner on 31 March 1979.

13. "When it's cruel to be kind", *Straits Times*, 29 June 1982. More details can be found in Baey Lian Peck, "Drug Addiction Treatment and Rehabilitation Programmes in Singapore", SANA Occasional Papers No. 7, February–March 1980.

14. These were the Roman Catholic Church, the National Council of churches, the Hindu Endowments Board, Hindu Advisory Board, Majlis Ugama Islam Singapura, Majlis Pusat Pertubuhan Budaya Melayu Singapura, Sikh Advisory Board, the Central Sikh Temple and the Inter-Religious Organisation. See "Religious groups back SANA aftercare services", *Straits Times*, 23 August 1977.

15. "74pc of former addicts have no aftercare, says SANA", *Straits Times*, 4 December 1978.

16. See Kuala Lumpur Declaration of Non-Government Organisations against Drug Abuse, <http://www.ifngo.org/main/pmwiki.php?n=IFNGO.KualaLumpurDeclaration>.

Chapter 3

SEEING THE BIGGER PICTURE

I was appointed Justice of the Peace in 1979.[1] I am still a JP. As you may know, a JP is appointed by the Prime Minister's Office through the Ministry of Home Affairs. Now, when I am eighty years old, a lot of my time is used advising young couples and marrying them. I take that job very seriously, as you might expect.

There are two or three tasks a JP has the authority to carry out. Of course, there are some other things you have to do as well, for example, when the registrar of the subordinate court allocates cases for mediation to you. Mediation is held in chamber at the Subordinate Court on Havelock Road. I have been happy with this position because of the connection it allows me to have with common people. My other positions — in SCORE, SANA, the HDB, St John or NTUC FairPrice — have all given me a deep understanding of the problems faced by Singaporeans, which comes in useful in my position as a JP.

For instance, I have sometimes to ask the lawyers in mediation cases that have been allocated to me to leave the chamber. With all due respect to them, lawyers are always in a fighting mode. I prefer having a discussion with only the two parties directly.

Their problems can be issues such as someone placing a flower pot at the common corridor. This leads to a neighbour who knows the rules regulating that to call the Town Council to complain. The council responds, and things get personal. Pride is hurt, egos are bruised. So, as JP, I have to talk them to their senses, deflate their egos with practical and economic considerations such as the costs of a civil suit.

Most of these cases involve young people, who seem easily offended nowadays, who know their rights, and who tend to get a bit too cocky too quickly.

Nevertheless, I love mediating. I take my time with them, getting to know the situation, and convincing them about what I think is best. With lawyers around, you cannot convince anybody in a peaceful manner. With them, it is about winning, not about getting along.

Even here, my work is voluntary. I don't do it for money. It's all national service. In the beginning, I had two sessions a quarter as a rule. Now, I have four sessions, each of these involving four cases.

I do solemnization as well. That's also done free of charge, except for transport charges, which I don't bother to get them to reimburse anyway. What I do in such matters is to ask for details. For example, if I think their income is too low, I advise them to wait until they are earning better before they get married. I ask about their housing situation. Are they renting, or are they staying with their parents?

When I find conditions not appropriate, I usually decline from further involvement in the case. I tell the couple why. I do not want to have to worry about them breaking up because of the reasons I explained to them already from the start. You see, a lot of family problems start with money, whether we like to think so or not. They can then get another JP to solemnize and marry them, if they do not wish to listen to my advice. As for me, I have done my job.

In the early days, when they gave me an *hong bao*, a red packet with money, I would take out the money, give it back to them, and keep the red packet only. Later on, after I came into contact with the Goddess of Mercy Pavilion in Tanjong Katong, I started a charity company called Mi Le Tian Rehabilitation Limited, named after the Laughing Buddha. K.S. Rajah and I were the first two directors. The objective of this company is to heal people. It does not do business or make money. So now, my solemnization fee is for the couple to donate to Mi Le Tian. In the beginning, some were donating a pittance, so I had to put a lower limit on the donations — at least $200, I would say. For Europeans, I ask for a larger sum. The official receipt that the charity company hands out for the donation goes to them.

Some give double or triple of what I ask them to give. Sometimes they still insist on giving me something anyway — another *hong bao* or a bottle of wine. But I still hand these over to Mi Le Tian. This is what I do now, three times per day, twice a week. I meet these couples several times, I tell them about the Women's Charter and about rules, rights and privileges.

Looking back, I am amazed at what I have managed to accomplish over the years. I am not trying to be ostentatious. No doubt I did read a lot and study hard despite my few years of schooling, and working with my father taught me an awful lot. His company was actually the first import-export company owned and run by a local back in those days. The others were all owned by foreigners.

I got more done in my life — and experienced more fulfilment — than I could ever have thought possible in the beginning, and I do believe today that there was a greater purpose to my life all along. Building up SCORE, through which I could help prisoners make the most of their time in detention and prepare them for a useful life after their release, was a big thing for me. Working so hard with NTUC Welcome, for the simple purpose of keeping prices low enough so that common Singaporeans would not suffer, was also highly gratifying. Helping the thousands of drug addicts out of their suffering through my work with the drug committee and with SANA was also a great joy.

After all these years, I am an expert at starting up statutory boards and the like. But seriously, what is required is staying power. One must stay for at least five years in anything one gets into, and see things through the teething stage. From then on, things tend to be alright.

Some of the events in my life that I can only call miraculous are hard to explain. They were not about me, I see now. They were about me as a conduit for greater powers at work. The drug treatment programme that came to me in the middle of the night was one of them. That was an act of the Almighty, as was the idea to recruit the religious institutions into aftercare for addicts.

I see now that any trouble in the world starts in your own mind. How you take things that happen to you is decisive. No doubt I have always been a Buddhist, but I did go to a Methodist school, and I know the Bible well. In my work with addicts, I would often use quotes from the Bible. The Buddhists don't have any objection to that at all. When working with SANA, and having contact with all the main religions, it was very helpful to be a Buddhist because Buddhism is a religion that is not declaratory.

I now think that my life has been about healing, bridging gulfs; about helping souls in distress, be they criminals or drug addicts, or simply poor; about advising young couples before they take the serious step into matrimony. The world is full of suffering that can be lessened through a show of creative compassion.

I have had a very active life, in all ways. I was always very healthy, always sporty, playing badminton and squash regularly. In fact, I have been jogging for the last forty-five years. I considered myself a retiree already when I became a member of the Housing & Development Board over forty years ago. I felt I was giving back to society, and was helping the state, which at that time was not very rich.

I was involved in the starting up of most of these organizations. That is quite different from — and certainly much harder than — just taking over an already established entity that already has a staff. At times, I was working sixteen hours a day.

I did all this because I love my country, because I had the skills and connections needed, and because I had already made my fortune early in life. So, I could not appreciate being brushed aside by people who had no idea about how to make things work, and what the necessary human qualities involved actually are.

It made me boiling mad in those days. But now, as I grow more and more philosophical, I am less upset by it. You see, I looked up to Dr Toh Chin Chye as a mentor who taught me a lot about the civil service and how I cannot be too careful where money is concerned. No doubt he was an abrasive and difficult character but he was kind at heart. He had a very sharp tongue, no doubt about that. Just like Lim Kim San, Dr Toh would say things as he saw them, even to Lee Kuan Yew.

For some reason, Dr Toh took a special liking to me. We once met on a plane. I was in first class, he was in economy. He came over and joked about what the trouble was with business types like me who could travel so well while he had to fly cheaply.

Throughout my life, I did not put much emphasis on being a Buddhist. It was a way of life, a way of thinking for me. When I really retired about five or six years ago, I became more involved in it. After I became a vegetarian, I began to understand things more and more; why humility is essential, and why the Confucian values of loyalty and filial piety are so important to social life. This ties in nicely with the Freemasons, who highlight Benevolence, Charity and Brotherly Love. Our charity works are never publicized, just as is the case with Buddhism.

Now, let me tell you more about Guanyin Ge, the Goddess of Mercy Pavilion. I came in touch with it several years ago. For health reasons, I had started taking Art of Living classes. They teach you how to breathe, basically. Our body is comprised of cells, and our cells live on oxygen. When we breathe well, we supply oxygen to these cells. They benefit from this, resulting in us being healthier and more attentive to life. It's as simple as that.

Now, I am someone who has worked with prisoners and addicts, and I have had a lot of dealings with all sorts of purported healers who wished to have access to these people. In short, I am a very sceptical person where such things are concerned. It was partly to please my wife that I went along to these classes.

The day before we were to leave for Chiangmai to attend an advanced course, the cornea in my left eye suffered a tear. This can get rather irritating; you see a flickering of light at the corner of your eye every now and then. My wife had had the same problem before, and she fixed that through laser treatment. So of course, I thought we should skip the course while I went to have my eye looked at. But my wife said that we should go to Chiangmai nevertheless: "Who knows, maybe they can help you."

So my wife and I, and my son Henry, went. The course took place over five days. Men and women were separated, and no talking was allowed for the first three days. One was not supposed to write to each other but most did. I was with my son and I did. Over the next few days, we would do our yoga, our breathing exercises. I would concentrate on channelling attention and energy to my left eye. Now, believe it or not, on the third day, the flickering light disappeared and has not come back since. After that, I believed in the exercise, as a healing process, not as a religion.

One day, an instructor from the Art of Living course came over to my house. Believe it or not, he said that my old friend, the late abbot of the Kong Meng San Temple, wanted to talk to me. This abbot and I had had a lot of disagreements in the old days when I was helping him to set up a functioning financial and administration system for the temple. But he had died a long time before, so you can imagine my amazement. This man from the Art of Living was now telling me that this dead man wanted to talk to me. He explained that the abbot was conveying his message through a lady. Being the sceptical person I am, I immediately replied, "Alright, we can go, but let's go immediately, this very moment. No need to make an appointment, no need to call ahead, let's go now."

I actually felt I should arrest this lady for cheating. So we took the car from our home at The Caribbean, my wife and I and this instructor, and we drove to see this lady.

She was surprised and had not expected us, which was my point. But curiously enough, the conversations I had that day with the lady were about things that were so intimate that no one else other than the abbot and myself could have known about them. It just had to be the abbot! No one could have known about it. I believe it was him, my wife believes it was him as well. That was when I realized how we humans are actually guided throughout our lives. I was guided all the way through all the things I did, and should not take personal credit for anything I did. And that was how I became much more involved in spiritual things. Things did happen in my life, while I was working with SANA and other places, which I cannot but call miracles. I mentioned all these earlier. I had always felt that something greater was at work than I could imagine or comprehend, but I did not see the full picture. I had never believed in supernatural forces acting in such a concrete manner, at least not until about five years ago.

Since then, I have become what one would have to call religious. Religion became a way of life for me. And, of course, once you enter that state of mind, the religion becomes a great part of your life, and you become much more philosophical in your outlook. Buddhism has opened my eyes; it has taught me a lot. If I had seen things then the way I do now, I suppose I would have done some of the things I did earlier in a better way. Many of the things I did were done in ignorance.

At certain points in one's life, things happen to push you in a new direction. I even began learning Mandarin after joining Guanyin Ge. Its teaching is all about light from Heaven. We are all born through light, and when we die, the light goes back to heaven. In the interim, we have a body, and it is used to help people, to serve mankind. It's as simple as that. In the group involved with the Guanyin Ge, you will find Catholics, Hindus, you name it.

I am glad that when our kids were young, we sent them to a Buddhist Sunday school. In fact, I read in the news recently that my son Henry is now the president of the Buddhist Fellowship. I am very happy about that. He had not told me, you see. He and his children are very supportive of me. The two boys are teenagers now, and on Sundays, they go to an old folks' home to help push people around in wheelchairs. It is all very commendable.

Now, I have observed that the majority of the patients in hospices in Singapore suffer from cancer. These are people who are terminally ill. To fight their pain, morphine is administered, and these people soon become addicted to the drug. But with our Holy Water, we can actually ease the pain without resorting to any drug. We actually have cancer cases with total remission. Our objective now is to recruit good people who can help the organization grow, either through voluntary work or donations. I am the chairman of the pavilion now, and my wife goes there every Tuesday and Thursday to help out with the cooking. On Tuesdays, we have teaching sessions and we have testimonials on Thursdays. Everything is recorded and archived. Every message that comes down through the lady is taped. There are thousands, tens of thousands, of them.

We recently built a three-storey museum in China, in one of the poorest villages there. It is in a very remote place, but within a year, we received a visit from representatives of the Tourist Attraction Board of China. They are considering declaring our museum a tourist spot. It lies in the middle of a valley in an area called Lotus Mountain because the surrounding hills form an embracing ring like a lotus flower around it. On the request of the Goddess of Mercy, we built it at a cost of S$1.5 million. It is quite inaccessible, but it is always packed with visitors. A flight from Singapore to Xiamen takes four hours. From Xiamen to the museum takes another fourteen hours — twelve hours by train and two hours by road. The museum has fifty-six pillars, and was completed in ten months, which is a great achievement in itself. On top of each of the fifty-six pillars is a Merlion, so it's a Singapore museum in a sense. I am its chairman.

I became a vegetarian about five years ago, and what I experienced was that after about four years, I became very sensitive to things happening and existing around me. I am also more forgiving now, I notice.

Guanyin Ge believes that there are roving spirits going around harming people without karma. For the last five years, I have been waking up at 5.30 in the morning to take a walk down to Keppel Island. Keppel Island, as you may know, was where massacres were carried out by the Japanese during the Second World War. Besides, there are many who have drowned there. So I had been going through the ritual of sprinkling Holy Water knowing that I could liberate these unhappy souls and send them off to Heaven, to a better place.

For the first four years, I did this as a ritual of belief. But over the last year, I have been able to see them, and even hear them. I discussed this with Niang Niang, this lady who is the embodiment of Guanyin. On her advice, I decided that I should not intrude into the area too early in the morning. No point tempting fate. So, I now go just at dawn, around 6.45 in the morning. Otherwise, it can be like walking into a bazaar, into a crowded place on the beach.

Things do hang together throughout one's life. I am reminded of how the treatment programme came to me. In a flash, I had all the details that I merely needed to write down. Today, I believe that my path, going through the Metrication Board, SANA, SCORE, NTUC FairPrice and others, was sort of preparing me to help mankind, to lessen suffering, to heal sick people. Doing good is self-generating. It is karma. All my life, I had been trying to do this.

I believe this new sensitivity comes from me becoming a vegetarian and helping people. Niang Niang said this is because my Third Eye is now open, and I can see into this world. The spiritual is all around us. Unless you are sensitive, you do not see them, both the good and the bad.

Over the last five years, I have seen countless miraculous things happen around Niang Niang, and at the Guanyin Ge. Unbelievable, uncanny things, hundreds of them, happening because of the power of the Holy Water — Shengming Guang, the Water of Life.

In this world, there are lots of things happening that we cannot understand. But I am now very happy. I have a good family. I am not in need of anything. I am content. For young people, I would like to highlight the importance of family. If you discard your family, if you don't believe in your family, then it's very difficult for you to get anywhere. You have to respect your parents. They have done more things for you than you can ever appreciate. You must also understand the importance of discipline, and always bear in mind the interest of the country.

It may be appropriate, given the nature of my life and my long participation in statutory boards and the like, to end with some words on the future of my beloved country, Singapore.

I do have a few worries, which I suppose, are strongly interrelated. Let me approach this by talking about migration first. We are taking in a lot of immigrants at the moment. There are strong national economic reasons for this. However, in the long term, this holds a threat to the common discipline found among Singaporeans. Foreigners may not adopt an anchored perspective on Singapore's special situation, and may only take the good and not the bad. This is related to economics, of course. Economics touch every aspect of our life. We do need foreigners. They will come, they will work here, become permanent residents, become citizens. We cannot stop them, and that in itself is not a problem at all. The problem lies in the added pressure on the integrity of our government and its officials. In the future, we will require more than ever, an incorruptible and competent state (see Appendices IX and X).

This is my biggest worry.

If the head degenerates, it will be felt below, and the degeneration spreads. I have always felt, and I have said this to foreigners who ask me what it is that makes Singapore tick, that it is because we have managed to contain corruption so well. Lee Kuan Yew has been a Rock of Gibraltar on that score. Compare us to China, and you see that the difference is the level of corruption. China has all the talents and the resources it needs to excel on all fronts. The thing holding it back is corruption.

What worries me now is, I am seeing cracks in our system. These cracks have to be fixed very quickly. The top must not compromise on this. I remember when I was at SCORE, my deputy, Quek Shi Lei, the Director of Prisons, called to say that my stepbrother had been nabbed for taking drugs and he was in a drug rehabilitation centre. My immediate reply to him was: "Do to him exactly what you would do to anyone else."

No special treatment for relatives. That is the attitude we must have. Around that time, a prominent politician called me up to say his son or grandson or some relative had been caught and could I do something about it. I just told him the story of my stepbrother being caught. He became silent. You have to be above board always. If you have small cracks in your armour, then people will come at you. Once you compromise, the cracks will get bigger and bigger.

One cannot live on the past accomplishments of the party and the government. The new leadership, whoever they are, will have to earn their place. There is no other way. The young are more knowledgeable, more outspoken, and they want to imitate foreign lifestyles, even if these, in most cases in my view, are wrong. But the young don't understand this and they like to think that they are right.

Perhaps we need to inculcate in the young an understanding of the past, and of the many innovative policies that lie behind the country's success.

Note

1. This was on 28 July 1979. See "21 are made Justices of the Peace", *Sunday Times*, 29 July 1979.

APPENDICES

APPENDIX I

"Letter to Myself", by Baey Lian Peck,
written on 27 May 1957

Letter to myself

41-24, Lengkong Satu,
Off Jalan Kembangan,
Singapore 14
27th May 1957

Dear Baey,

When you open this letter, you will be nearly 46 years old, and married for 21 years. If God permits, you will have children of your own, and soon hope to be a grandfather, as your dear wife Daisy, is now pregnant and will be having a baby in the middle of the next month.

The reason for this letter to yourself is that you are almost certain that you will succeed in business, and that the Company, Baey Kim Swee & Co Ltd, will be ever bigger and prosperous, not only in this line, but in all the field of commerce, and that you might be swell-headed (like your father) and put all the glory to yourself, instead of to the other people who helped you to succeed.

Should you succeed, and be much more wealthier than your father, you promised that you will be generous and helpful not only to your relations but to the people, whom you made your money from. You would not make the mistakes your father made, by taking all the credits and blaming the bad and unsuccessful on other people.

By now, some of your children would be in school, and you promised to give them a good education, girl or boy alike, so that they will be able to [fend] for themselves in later years. Although you wish them to follow your footstep in business, you must not force them, if they wish to take up any other type of professions.

You promised not to have second wife, because of your unhappy childhood days due to the two stepmothers, and your own mother being kicked out by your father.

You know that it is impossible to be entirely faithful to Daisy, but you promised to yourself that should you ever feel tempted by woman, you will pay them with money (or other ways) for the enjoyment. But you will never marry a second wife, so that your children will not suffer as you have suffered.

If you are rich, and have succeeded in reaching your ambition, that is: a millionaire with steady income from your many investments, you would not forget your friends and relations, and would endeavour your utmost to help them.

You must not be dominating, and you must not be like your father in your family life. Your children should be encouraged to discuss with you their problems, and be able to joke with you.

If any of your children falls in love, you would not be too hard-headed, but listen to your wife and friends whom you should seek advice. Remember the Chinese proverb: There are successful *chongquan* students but no *chongguan* teachers so never think you are more clever than your children, because time marches on, and your ideas may be old fashion and out-of-date.

You promised your wife Daisy, that you would build her a house with a library, children rooms, carpeted floor, beautiful furniture, French windows with long curtains if you have not already done so. You also promised to let her have a business of her own (for example, a dress making shop which you will help to run, but she's the boss) and provided her with a car of her own.

All the above are written on your first wedding Anniversary, and that you purposely wrote those things to remind yourself, after [having] talked over with your wife in bed. It is 12 o'clock midnight; the 27th of May 1957 has just passed.

Yours
Baey Lian Peck

P.S.

Should you still [be] struggling to reach your ambition, do not give up, try harder for there are so many people who have confidence in you. The most important of all, you have to help your brothers and sisters and they are depending on you. You promised your wife that you will not give up trying, and you will die trying, if you fail to reach your ambition.

APPENDIX II

"Singapore checks inflation's rise", *Straits Times*, 11 September 1978

Singapore's current inflation rate is the highest in three years. But there is no cause for alarm as the price increase here is among the lowest in the world.

Latest figures from the International Monetary Fund show that the nation's inflation is running lower than three of its Asean partners and its arch Asian export rival, South Korea and Taiwan.

Also, the rise in consumer prices is slower than the average of the industrialised nations.

For the first seven months of this year, the nation's consumer price index, according to government statistics, rose by 5.3 per cent which is higher than increases for the past three years.

IMF statistics show that the annual increase of Singapore's consumer prices for April is 5.1 per cent against 7.2 per cent for the Philippines, 9.1 per cent for Thailand, and 10.9 per cent for Indonesia. April figures for Malaysia are not available yet.

The inflation rates for Taiwan and South Korea are 8 per cent and 12.4 per cent respectively.

The consumer price rise for 14 industrialised nations averages 6.4 per cent, reports the IMF. These countries are the US, Canada, Japan, Britain, Switzerland, West Germany, Italy, Holland, Sweden, France, Austria, Belgium, Denmark and Norway.

Economists have predicted that Singapore's consumer prices will rise between $4\frac{1}{4}$ and $5\frac{1}{4}$ per cent for the whole of this year. Last year, the CPI increased by 3.2 per cent.

The main reasons for the hike in local consumer prices this year are increases in the cost of food, transport and miscellaneous items such as medical fees and cinema admission charges.

The barmy days of rock-bottom inflation rates in Singapore (consumer prices rose at annual rates of not more than 2 per cent in the 1960s and early 1970s) ended when prices soared to 22.9 per cent in 1973 and 22.3 per cent in 1974. Without a doubt, the oil crisis triggered off spiralling inflation in the world economy. But its underlying causes stemmed from the lack of world financial discipline, resulting in deficit financing and easy credit creation, something which had been going on for two decades.

The 1950s and 1960s saw the emergence of the inflation-prone consumer society of US and other parts of the world.

Cheaper

That was a period of increasing private consumption, higher aspirations and rising incomes, which generated stronger demand for consumer durables.

Cheaper air fares boosted tourism, pushing up demand for hotels, restaurants, airports, and roads.

More emphasis on advertising moulded consumer attitudes and opened new vistas for merchandising products.

The Korean and the Vietnam wars led to heavy military spending by the US, with its ramifications for other parts of the world. Furthermore, governments in many nations embarked on expansionary and fiscal policies.

The combination of these factors sparked inflation which ravaged the world economy in 1974 and 1975.

But tough anti-inflation measures adopted by industrialised nations and Singapore's own economic policies combined to dampen prices, resulting in the local CPI rising by only 2.6 per cent in 1976. Since then, prices have remained stable here.

The big jump in local prices in 1974 and 1975 stemmed mainly from imported inflation in the form of higher import prices of goods and increased freight costs.

But there were local causes too. Rapid economic expansion in the 1960s and 1970s led to heavy spending by the Government and private sectors. The nation's political and economic stability attracted large capital inflows from abroad.

Fast economic growth and a marked slowdown in population growth led to full employment and then labour shortages, resulting in upward pressure on wages.

The inflationary situation in the mid-1970s was also aggravated by profiteering by local traders.

But inflationary pressures levelled off because of the setting up of the National Wages Council, establishment of Welcome supermarkets and the government build-up of rice stockpiles and adoption of effective monetary and fiscal policies.

Economists have dismissed the prospects of Singapore returning to the negligible inflation rates of the 1960s and early 1970s during the next few years. But at the same time, they ruled out the possibility of Singapore reliving the nightmarish days of 1973 and 1974.

They forecast local consumer prices going up between 3 and 7 per cent annually during the next few years.

Last year, the inflation rate in the OECD group of nations was 7.9 per cent. OECD economists have a rate of $7\frac{1}{4}$ per cent for this year and 7 per cent for the first half of next year. — *Business Times*.

Note: Reproduced with permission of Singapore Press Holdings.

APPENDIX III

Queries by Baey Lian Peck at the board meeting of Intraco Ltd, 29 April 1986

QUERIES BY MR. BAEY LIAN PECK AT THE BOARD MEETING OF INTRACO LIMITED
HELD AT 456 ALEXANDRA ROAD, SINGAPORE 0511 ON 29TH APRIL 1986 AT 9.30 AM
==

1. The Chairman had stated in the last Board Meeting held on 25th of
    March 1986 that in his opinion, insufficient provisions were made
    for dimunition in value of investment, trade and intercompany owings.
    Consequently, the amended copy of the "audited financial accounts"
    has been downward adjusted. Would the Chairman please explain:

    A) What is the basis for the additional provision for dimunition
        in value of investment of S$1,136,000.00?

    B) What is the basis for the additional provision for dimunition
        of "owings" by subsidiaries of $1,262,000.00?

    C) What is the basis for the additional provision for dimunition
        of doubtful debts of S$2,790,000.00?

2. Is the Chairman aware of the additional "notation" in the Accoun-
    ting Policy of the Company, under paragraph (E) Trade Debtors, as
    follows:

        Trade Debtors are stated after specific and general pro-
        visions for doubtful debts. General provision is created
        for the first time this year.

3. Is the Chairman aware that this paragraph was not mentioned in
    the previous "draft" audited financial report presented at the
    25th of March 1986 meeting, which he rejected as insufficient
    provisions for dimunition in value of investment, trade and
    intercompany owings?

4. I would like to draw attention to the Directors Report, paragraph
    5, b (ii) in page 4 which states:

        At the date of this report, the Directors are not aware
        of any circumstances which could render:

        "THE VALUES ATTRIBUTED TO CURRENT ASSETS MISLEADING"

5. Is the Chairman aware of Government's intention to dispose off its
    holding in Intraco at the appropriate time?

6. Is the Chairman aware of any party who have expressed an interest
    in the purchase of Government's share holding?

7. In the light of Government's privatisation policy, does the Chair-
    man not agree that the presentation of the Company's assets and
    statement of accounts other than an "accurate" one, could possibly
    be construed as an attempt to mislead the public in general and
    the Shareholders in particular?

BAEY LIAN PECK J.P. B.B.M.
29TH APRIL 1986.

APPENDIX IV

Offer by Morgan Grenfell (Asia) Ltd for the acquisition of Intraco Ltd shares, 26 June 1986

THIS DOCUMENT IS IMPORTANT AND REQUIRES YOUR IMMEDIATE ATTENTION. PLEASE READ IT CAREFULLY.

If you are in doubt about this Document, you should consult your stockbroker, bank manager, solicitor or other professional adviser. Morgan Grenfell (Asia) Limited is acting on behalf of United Industrial Corporation Limited and does not purport to advise shareholders of Intraco Limited.

If you have sold all your ordinary shares in the capital of Intraco Limited, you should at once hand this Document and the accompanying Form of Acceptance and Transfer to the purchaser or to the bank, stockbroker or agent through whom you effected the sale for transmission to the purchaser.

Offer by

MORGAN GRENFELL (ASIA) LIMITED

on behalf of

UNITED INDUSTRIAL CORPORATION LIMITED

(Incorporated in the Republic of Singapore)

to acquire all the issued ordinary shares
of $1.00 each fully paid in the capital of

INTRACO LIMITED

(Incorporated in the Republic of Singapore)

other than those already owned by
UNITED INDUSTRIAL CORPORATION LIMITED

ACCEPTANCES SHOULD BE RECEIVED BY 12.00 NOON ON 18TH JULY 1986 OR SUCH LATER DATE OR DATES AS MAY BE ANNOUNCED BY UNITED INDUSTRIAL CORPORATION LIMITED.

The procedure for acceptance is set out on page 6.

This Document is dated 26th June 1986.

APPENDIX V

A report written by W. Clifford, Director of the Australian
Institute of Criminology, following a study of Singapore's
correctional rehabilitation, sent on 18 January 1978

**Productivity — The Key to Singapore's Correctional
Rehabilitation**

Singapore's approach to both corrections and its drug problems
is positive and direct. For that reason its policies are either lauded
as sensible or criticised as repressive according to the
commentators' own position on the current drug and correctional
controversy. Like most other countries, Singapore is not yet able
to show that any one policy rather than another has been
conspicuously successful: and even if it did claim success there
would doubtless be scope for varying interpretations of this
according to the criteria used. If one begins however with the
modest assumptions that the people responsible for policy in
Singapore are neither unlettered nor uncultured, that they are
widely travelled and alive to the developments on corrections
and drug problems in other countries of the world — and that
they are genuinely concerned about the best interests of their
country, then it is possible to identify objectives and tease out
the principles for some future evaluation.

There are two arms to Singapore's action to deal with drugs
and crime: and the policy is gradually to bring these together in
a pincer movement to improve rehabilitation. One arm is the
country's drive to develop, socially and economically. There is a
keen appreciation of Singapore's need to be competitive in exports
and to serve as an international market. With two million people
crowded on about 600 square kilometres which offer little except
human resources, secondary industry, tourism [and] commerce

loom large as means of survival and improvement in the quality of life. Singapore is sensitive to the fact that it must produce and market on competitive terms to earn its foreign currency. It has therefore sought to mobilise the relatively unused human resources in the prisons and in the rehabilitation centres to provide selected competitive exports. The second arm of correctional and drug policy is the personal rehabilitation of the inmates of institutions with a corresponding reduction in the rates of recidivism. The attempt to join these two arms into a total thrust to benefit both the community and the individual is well illustrated by the creation of SCORE — the Singapore Corporation of Rehabilitative Enterprises. This statutory body is chaired by an industrialist, Mr Baey Lian Peck, who is a successful entrepreneur in his own right and who practically gives his services to the government. It was decided that public servants whether prison staff or educated and enlightened administrators were unlikely to understand the private industrial sector so that Mr Baey was asked to take over and develop the work. Under his guidance, the prisons and drug rehabilitation centres are being industrialised. Mr Baey Lian Peck holds other posts which are relevant and significant for this new development of correctional and rehabilitative services. He is Chairman of a government committee on the treatment and rehabilitation of drug addicts and president of a voluntary body, the Singapore Anti Narcotics Association. In SCORE, the Chairman's Chief Executive Officer is Mr Quek Shi Lei who is also Director of Prisons — which includes responsibility for institutions dealing with the reform of young offenders and even the senior approved schools.

SCORE works on the principle that the older concept of vocational training in the prisons (which incidentally already marketed a wide range of rattan and other products) did not greatly benefit the offender. He was unlikely to follow the trade he had learned in prison when he was released and might indeed have been handicapped in a swiftly changing commercial situation if his prison training made [him so] highly specialised as a tailor, shoemaker or carpenter that he could not adapt. The new idea therefore is that the offender should be trained to maximise his profitability as a worker in any local employment situation. He is taught, in the process of the industrialisation of the institution, to make comparisons between his productivity and that of other workers and to learn how to make more money by analysing the demand for his services and offering himself in any capacity which will bring him a greater return.

The industrialisation of the prisons and the drug rehabilitation centres was sold as an idea to private firms. At first none of them wished to get involved in prison services especially by investing their own funds: but by propagating the idea that greater profit could be obtained by paying inmates two thirds of the prevalent wages outside, a number of companies were induced by SCORE to invest their own capital to install [a] factory plant inside the prisons or centres, converting to line production where necessary the older institutional workshops. The firms enter this work for profit — not directly to rehabilitate prisoners. The inmates represented by SCORE are also in it for profit. With productivity as the motive therefore and with the constraints applied by the need to be internationally competitive, both sides co-operate in a venture, which SCORE believes, enhances the dignity of labour, takes any welfare taint from the work for prisoners, avoids patronising them and allows them to develop their own business on the basis of being able to compete in the labour market.

One might expect union or private sector objections to "unfair" competition since the wages paid by producers with factories in prisons are one third lower than those which would have to be paid for non-institutional labour. However the

Chairman himself represents the attitude of private firms, there seems to be no organised protest and indeed a local readiness to applaud the idea of the prisons becoming more self-supportive. Moreover the Chairman of SCORE, in another capacity, is also Chairman of the organisation of [National] Trade Union Co-operatives which have a number of enterprises aimed at increasing exports and bringing costs down. He explains that the Singapore philosophy is not only for unions to demand more for less but to benefit the employee by making his wages go further. Last year there was no inflation and indeed the cost of living slightly decreased: this year inflation has reached only 2 per cent. Whether due to the interconnections represented by the Chairman or not, SCORE does not yet seem to have attracted any serious private or union opposition to its introduction of prison labour into the market.

The inmate is paid rather less than the outside worker but sometimes his conditions are better. Naturally he is being fed and housed and, although he contributes from his pay towards this, he could be argued to be receiving a sum roughly equal to the third less than average wages outside, which he receives.

Again, regulations in Singapore require an assembly line employee to have at least a space of four square metres for his work. In private industry this requirement is frequently evaded — but not in the prisons or centres: here a worker gets at least the minimum space and usually is given much more. An inmate is eligible for promotion to supervisory positions as his skill increases. To ensure production standards the firm running the prison or centre factory — usually for the production of electronic good which are exported — brings in its own production engineers or specialists and quality control supervisors who check the finished article. These people come to the prison or centre daily and work alongside the inmates. As inmates improve however they are frequently able to do the job as well as — and sometimes even better than these factory employees: so that when and if vacancies occur the firm may prefer to promote an inmate to the position rather than bring in outside labour. Released prisoners who have become skilled are also employed by the firm as outside labour and stay at the work in the prison factory although they go home at night. Here, it should be noted, advantage is being taken of the size of Singapore. Usually there is no great distance between homes and prisons.

The aim being rehabilitation and the prevention of recidivism there is great emphasis upon the work available for the prisoner or inmate on his release. Community rehabilitation is also important because, with the rapid construction in Singapore of late, a person who is in an institution for three years may find the entire district in which he was born and previously lived, razed to the ground to provide land for other types of development. His family is rehoused with people who are strangers so that on his release he is not returning to an environment he knows. For such reasons his hope of being able to continue working with the firm which employed him in the institution is very important because it provides continuity not only of work but of a lifestyle. But, where released inmates are not taken on by the firm or do not wish to continue in the same employment, SCORE will help them to join with other released offenders in the organisation of their own co-operative to produce for themselves or to do work on a sub-contracted basis for other firms. If a person released decides to do none of these things but to make his own way after release he is free to do so. In this case the idea is to ensure that whilst employed inside the institution he has acquired an entrepreneur attitude to the sale of his labour or the organisation of his affairs: the intention is to equip each and everyone with the right incentives, with the know-how to exploit his abilities to his own best advantage in the labour market. He is helped for example to look for that kind of work in which an income can be earned simply because no one wants to do it and is prepared to pay highly for it to be done. It may mean taking on cleaning work, driving, delivery services. It may mean applying for work on the second shift of a day. This second shift is not popular in factories and there are usually vacancies. The concept is to help him to think productively. An idea just now being considered for a project is for prisoners or inmates to be selected to form co-operatives whilst inside the institutions and to tender for contracts to do the "dirty" work outside e. g. garbage collection, builders, labourers. This might run into union trouble later but there is confidence that it will not if the jobs selected are those that no one else wants to do. Always the inmate with an eye to his best use of himself on release is being encouraged to make his own openings.

How is it all working? These are early days. SCORE has been going for less than two years: but already it has made an impact. The prisons and centres in which vocational training was frequently regarded as time filling or as being purely training have become veritable hives of activity: this, it is said, has greatly reduced discipline problems and vastly improved morale. There is a sense of purpose. It is also clear that the country is benefiting from the exports; the firms involved are quite satisfied with results and their productivity exceeds that which they have in external enterprises. There is great confidence being generated in the concept of aided self-help which the total project represents.

Still not clear however is whether this new undertaking within the prisons and the centres does in fact rehabilitate offenders on release and thereby reduce recidivism. A careful monitoring of the total scheme is in progress but several more years will be necessary before there can be a real evaluation.

It should be remembered that every young offender is visited by a social worker of the Social Welfare Department. On his admission to an institution, his family outside is visited: and then the same social worker follows his progress and his family relationships throughout the period of the sentence. In so far as possible, the same worker is available on his release to help him get settled, find work and deal with problems which inevitably arise on his release.

Thus the business-like approach of SCORE is reinforced by social support services to further develop the rehabilitative scheme. These days however when, in the West, there is a growing conviction that "nothing works" and that even the best forms of rehabilitation do not greatly reduce the recidivist rate, it is likely that aggregate figures may not reflect individual benefit. A number of case-studies in depth would be needed to amplify the statistics.

There has been United Nations encouragement to bring crime prevention more effectively into national development planning. SCORE is one example of the direction in which some countries might be interested in moving in order to do this. There will be great interest, therefore in Singapore's results.

APPENDIX VI

SCORE dinner speech by Chairman Baey Lian Peck at Cockpit Hotel on 31 March 1979

First, I would like to thank you for your presence. This will be the only occasion in which SCORE is holding a dinner on its own. We will be joining the Prisons Department when it holds its future annual dinners.

This evening is perhaps a good time to reflect on what objectives SCORE has set out to achieve, what are expected of the staff and what roles private enterprises can play.

SCORE's objectives, as they have often been stressed, are:

(i) To inculcate in inmates exact industrial discipline; and
(ii) To provide work to as many inmates as possible.

We have one aim; that is, to lead and rehabilitate those who have gone astray and try [to] turn them into useful citizens again.

The task of rehabilitation falls no less on the Prisons Department than on the staff of SCORE. Staff of SCORE must therefore share this responsibility in an enduring and positive manner. Working in a rehabilitative environment is more than a job. It is a public service. And we will be doing the public a great service if, through our collective efforts, we are able to inculcate in drug takers and prison inmates (particularly the recidivists), the will and determination to reform themselves.

We have done quite well over the last 2 years but there is no cause for [rejoicing] yet. We still have much more to do in the years ahead. It is the duty of the management to ensure that conditions of service for staff are competitive to Government departments and related industries in the private sector. Every officer must, however, demonstrate his or her commitment to the Corporation. In order that management can build up the infrastructure for a conducive working environment, it is important that there must be more feedback from staff on the ground level. The submission of fortnightly reports on workshops' performance, though a chore, is necessary so that experience from the workshop could be translated into effective policies.

SCORE is grateful to participating companies for their contributions to our work programme. While the viability of any investment is a prime concern of businessmen, companies should not look at their participation in SCORE solely from the business point of view. They should view it more as a public service. I hope, therefore, they can further assist us by expanding the factories they have already established in the prisons or DRCs and take in more inmates for production.

Finally, I would like to thank the Director of Prisons and his staff for rendering their co-operation promptly and unhesitatingly to SCORE. There may be occasions when the views of workshop officers differ from that of the workshop supervisors on inmates' conduct. But I am gratified that more often than not, such differences are merely different views of the same objective, i.e. the best way to inculcate the proper work discipline in the inmates.

Once again, I thank you for your presence and hope you enjoy your dinner.

APPENDIX VII

"A love that has lasted 54 years", by Sarah Ng and Jean Loo, *Sunday Times*, 28 May 2006

Businessman and community leader Baey Lian Peck was playing a game of badminton at his classmate's Grange Road home 54 years ago when he caught sight of his friend's sister and fell instantly in love.

The 21-year-old was so smitten with the 15-year-old student that he would drive her to school every day to make sure other admirers had no chance of winning her heart.

"It was love at first sight on my part. She's such a beautiful and caring girl, and she had many admirers. I was naturally worried," he told *The Sunday Times*.

Fifty years, four children and 13 granchildren later, they are still together.

Last night, Dr Baey and his wife, Daisy, celebrated 50 years of marriage with 600 guests, including President S R Nathan and Mrs Nathan, with a lavish dinner party at the Ritz-Carlton.

The couple founded American International Industries Group, the oilfield equipment company now run by their son, Henry, though Dr Baey still serves as chairman.

He has also sat on several government boards, served 19 years as president of the Singapore's Anti-Narcotics Association and was one of the founders of the NTUC FairPrice supermarket chain.

It's a far cry from the days when Mrs Baey's younger brother would chaperone the couple to Koek Road to eat porridge and ice kachang.

He popped the question — on a bench in a reservoir park one evening — two years into their courtship.

The couple married on May 27 in 1956 and threw a wedding dinner for about 300 guests in a Chinese restaurant in Middle Road.

Last night's dinner was a more multinational affair, attended by the couple's four children, a handful of government ministers and relatives, friends and business associates from Brunei, India, Malaysia, Portugal, Sri Lanka and the United States.

The night began with a video slideshow to the tune of Elvis Presley's Hawaiian Wedding Song, showing footage of their wedding in 1956.

Guests, decked out in tuxedos and flashy gowns, were full of admiration.

Mr Ricky Sim, chief operating officer of Suntec Investment Group, said: "They're one big happy family".

"It's excellent that they've managed to keep it going for 50 years".

After the guests had tucked into a sumptuous spread of barbecued suckling pig, shark's fin soup and braised abalone, a second montage video appeared, showing the couple's courtship, wedding, their children's formative years and, later, their grandchildren.

When the video showed Mrs Baey saying to her husband, "I will follow wherever you go," there was hardly a dry eye among the guests.

When asked the secret of their long marriage, both said: "Give and take".

Said Dr Baey: "We understand that we are not perfect and we give way to each other".

"It's not sacrifice but out of the love we have for each other".

Mrs Baey was more matter-of-fact.

"We are husband and wife and should stick together whether it's during successful or difficult times," she said.

Note: Reproduced with permission of Singapore Press Holdings.

APPENDIX VIII

Letter to Prime Minister Lee Hsien Loong calling for cross-subsidization as control measure on inflation, 9 February 2008

Prime Minister Lee Hsien Loong
Prime Minister's Office
Orchard Road
Istana
Singapore 238823

Dear Mr Lee,

May I begin this letter by wishing you and your family a Happy and Successful Lunar New Year.

In the midst of the so-called OPEC war in the mid-seventies when the price of oil escalated and inflation went wild, NTUC Welcome Consumer Co-operative, now known as NTUC FairPrice was set up to combat inflation in our country.

The late Mr Lim Kim San was Chairman Board of Trustees and I was Chairman Board of Directors as well as CEO.

Through a system of cross-subsidy by progressively reducing the prices of about a dozen essential items that had direct bearing on the cost of living of the workers and subsidized by profit margin from the rest of the other items, we were able not only to contain inflation but managed to get it reduced when inflation was rising elsewhere. Gradually, those essential items became loss leaders and because of competition, the other supermarkets and provision shops were compelled to adopt the same strategy. The attached article from the *Straits Times* of September 11, 1978 showing the inflation rate of Singapore and selected countries would give you an insight into the success of the system.

If you consider the system worth pursuing, I will be delighted to brief you further on the matter.

Yours respectively,

BAEY LIAN PECK
Encl. *Straits Times* article, September 11, 1978 [see APPENDIX II]

c.c. Minister Mentor Lee Kuan Yew.

Note: In the following week, Prime Minister Lee Hsien replied to thank Dr Baey for the advice while Minister Mentor Lee Kuan Yew's response was "Good work. Put it in NTUC News."

APPENDIX IX

Baey Lian Peck's advice to grandson Zhong Yi on the changing political scene in Singapore, through an e-mail exchange, 30 April 2011
At 08:56 PM 30/4/2011, Zhong Yi wrote:

Dear Kong Kong,

How are you? How is the family? i sent you 2 replys but im not sure if you received them. Anyways, i've been reading up and trying to follow up on the whole GE that's going on in Singapore. I was just curious as to what were your thoughts about the whole PAP/SDP thing going on. I don't really know much but to me hasn't the PAP done a good job so far? The SDP seems like they're trying to market themselves as a "people's government" but do you really think they'll be suitable? ...

Just thought i'd ask for your opinion plus i also miss you both so sending an email always helps

Lots of love
Zhong Yi

>>>>>>>>>>>>>>>>>>>>>>>>>>>>>>>>>>>>>

My Dear Grandson,

It is most gratifying to know that you are now able to vote in the forthcoming Singapore's General Election and what pleases me most is the fact that you are sufficiently interested and concerned in writing to me for my thoughts. You are being very wise. Though just only one vote, your vote may make a difference in securing the right political leader to help to chart our country's future.

If you had asked me this question when you were back here, I would have suggested that we meet over lunch or dinner as it would take at least a couple of hours to fully enlighten you on the pertinent facts and events from the time when we were a British Colony, through the three and a half years of Japanese Occupation and its subsequently surrender, leading to nationhood, initially as part of Malaysia and later into an independent sovereign nation under Lee Kuan Yew. Without knowing the past events, one would not be able to appreciate and comprehend the political, social and economic landscape that transformed our country into what it is today.

History tells us [about] the common desire of the masses to escape from poverty, hunger, tyranny, and corrupted or inefficient government that led to a country's evolution into an independent sovereign nation, where [a] citizen not only has a stake but freedom to participate in the country's development. However, this was not the case with Singapore in the beginning. In 1959, Singapore was given self-government status by the British Government and Lee Kuan Yew was the elected "Chief" Minister. The people [through] a referendum, chose independence by joining Malaysia rather than British rule. It would be too long for me to elaborate on the "why" and "how" the then Malaya agreed to accept Singapore as part of Malaysia in 1963; suffice to say that we were kicked out of Malaysia two years later due to political differences. Overnight, Singapore became a Sovereign and Independent nation under Lee Kuan Yew as prime minister. In other words, the future of Singapore was placed solely in the hands of Lee Kuan Yew and the PAP. Though some members subsequently broke away to set up an opposition party, but what is important was that the PAP prevailed and Lee Kuan Yew remained as prime minister.

It is a well established fact that the character of the Chief Executive is reflected in the organization that he heads and the same can be said of a Nation. Over the past 45 years under the leadership of Lee Kuan Yew, the country has had fantastic economic development and [a] progress second to none, but the way in which it was achieved has been a matter of grave contention. Over the period when he was Prime Minister, LKY had left his "mark", not only in the political and economic arena but also in the social lifestyle of the people.

There are now citizens who think that they have acquired sufficient political knowledge to change the style of government, hence you have the Workers Party, SDP. Reform Party, etc. You must remember that the duty of a Government is not to tell the people, including commerce and industry, what to do but rather to set up and manage necessary infrastructure so as to create opportunity for them to develop and excel.

I sincere believe that the quality of a good political leader is not only "knowledge" but more importantly, he must have "Loyalty", "Integrity", "Humility", "Compassion", "Morality" and a genuine desire to serve the people. These qualities cannot be bought or randomly acquired. They are the reflection of the innermost thoughts and conscience, in other words, the "character" of that person. The "family" is the safe depository of culture, custom, tradition and lifestyle and it is through the family that a child acquires such a "character". The "character forming age" is from the day a child is born up to about 7 to 12 years (school going age). This is why, the family is so important for it imparts "character" whereas school and university impart "knowledge". You will therefore see that it is better to have a person with [character] rather than [one] having a University Graduate without these qualities.

You will have to do some research to ascertain the "quality" of the person or persons in the SMC/GRC [to whom] you wish to give your vote. Remember, a person's position, rank and wealth are not signs of good character. I do not believe that the opposition would be able to gain sufficient seats to take over the Government. It would however be desirable to have some of them in Parliament to raise questions on important issues which otherwise might be swept under the carpet. Indications are that this time, there might be more opposition members elected.

The SDP under Dr. Chee has started off on the wrong foot. He is in a hurry to get nowhere and going to jail for whatever reason is not a good start.

Love

Kong Kong

APPENDIX X

Baey Lian Peck's advice to grandson Yi Wei on the changing political scene in Singapore through an e-mail exchange, 27 May 2011
Written at 01:49 AM 12/5/2011:

Dear Kongkong and ZY [Zhong Yi],

Not sure if you have seen this, but I just watched this short clip that my dad linked me to and felt that it was quite insightful. Thought to share it with everyone.

I share the same sentiments as ZY — hasn't the PAP been doing a decent job all these years? What is all this whining about?

Perhaps a reason why we think in this fashion is because we have been blessed with being "the fortunate lot" in Singapore. And although we probably do have some awareness of the less fortunate, we can never fully empathize with what they have to live with. According to this video, they are apparently quite oppressed. This makes a lot of sense — an economically driven country like ours putting less economically productive people at the bottom of the food chain. Or is that fallacy?

Just some food for thought.

http://english.aljazeera.net/programmes/101east/2011/05/20115494458152827.html

Love,
Yi Wei

>>>>>>>>>>>>>>>>>

Date: Fri, 27 May 2011 16:20:27 +0800
From: "Dr. Baey Lian Peck"
Subject: Re: Hello from Perth!

Dear Yi Wei,

What the PAP had achieved is water down the drain. Over time, people forget especially those who had not lived through the period of development. Politics like a family is a living thing, it has to change with the times. What is important is that the people who are asking for changes should fully understand the difficulties the country or organizations have gone through and try to put themselves in the same situations.

Take for example NTUC Welcome Consumers Co-operative Supermarkets. Dr Goh Keng Swee mooted the idea of a consumers' co-operative to combat the seemingly uncontrollable inflation due to [the] decision by OPEC (Organization of Oil Producing Countries) in the middle of nineteen seventies to increase the price of oil from $1.50 to $11.50 per barrel resulting in serious worldwide inflations, particularly in Singapore with no natural resources when prices of essential food shot up over 200% overnight. It was [then] that Mr Lim Kim San, the then finance minister, persuaded me to take over the chair of a Board of eminent directors, such as the former President of Singapore (deceased) Mr Ong Teng Cheong, the former Minister of National Development (deceased) Mr Teh Cheang Wan, the President of NTUC Mr Phey Yew Kok (now a fugitive), prominent bankers and others. With a paid up capital of $250,000.00 he instructed me (1) to combat the rising inflation, (b) be competitive and yet viable and (3) not to destroy the retailers in the process. To compound the matter, the merchants and wholesalers in the early days, were wary of the labour movement and were under the impression that NTUC Welcome was out to take over their business. You can imagine the difficulties NTUC Welcome had to face, not being able to establish strong relationships with wholesalers and suppliers for lower prices, the complain of higher prices by the consumers who were using our prices as a "check-price" with all retailers. It would [need] too long to elaborate further on the difficulties; suffice to say that everything was set up from scratch with unfriendly trading partners. Another problem is that the President of NTUC insisted that the objective of NTUC Welcome should be designed for the benefit of its members against [my objective that it should be] for all the people of Singapore. This fundamental disagreement led to the setting up of similar supermarkets called PIEU/SILO by NTUC. In most cases, [the] location of their supermarkets [was] nearby or next to those of NTUC Welcome. However, Mr. C.V. Devan Nair, the former President of Singapore who was then NTUC Secretary-General, continued to give me full support and encouragement. Fortunately for me, due to mismanagement, Mr. Phey, the President of NTUC absconded and NTUC Welcome was asked to take over PIEU/SILO and the name was changed to NTUC FairPrice in the middle of nineteen eighties. Inflation was checked and Singapore economy grew rapidly. It was then that I resigned and Mr Gopinath Pillai took over as Chairman.

I attached a *Straits Times* article titled NTUC pays tribute to "special 50" to highlight the points I raised in the first paragraph of this email. What was achieved in the past is water down the drain. The perception of the new generation is based on what they can see and read. Fighting inflation is in the past; what is important is the present where the growth and profits go to NTUC. With the task of fighting inflation over, NTUC FairPrice concentrated on making profit, like any other commercial enterprise. The above enumeration represents less than one percent of what actually transpired but I think it is sufficient to illustrate to you what I mean.

Love

Kong Kong

References

Primary Sources

PP — Private papers of Dr Baey Lian Peck and Biographical Record of Dr Baey Lian Peck, Chairman, American International Industries;

OH — Oral History Interview with Dr Baey Lian Peck, for the project, "The Civil Service — A Retrospection", by Santanu Gupta. Audiotaped on September–November 2008, in ten compact discs; Accession Number: 003339/10. Transcribed in June 2009 by Larry Loke and edited by Foo Kim Leng. Oral History Centre, National Archives of Singapore.

Secondary Sources

Baey Lian Peck. "Drug Addiction Treatment and Rehabilitation Programmes in Singapore". Occasional Papers No. 7. Singapore Anti-Narcotics Association, February–March 1980.

K.S. Rajah. "Drug Problems in Adolescents". Occasional Papers No. 3. Singapore Anti-Narcotics Association, 1979.

SCORE: A Decade of Dedication. Singapore: Singapore Corporation of Rehabilitative Enterprises, 1986.

Welcome Annual Reports 1974 to 1982.

SANA Annual Reports 1979 to 1995.

SANA Occasional Papers 1 to 12.

Internet Sites and Mass Media Sources

Straits Times, Singapore. NewspaperSG: <http://newspapers.nl.sg>.

New Nation. NewspaperSG: <http://newspapers.nl.sg>.

ABOUT THE AUTHOR

OOI KEE BENG is a Senior Fellow at the Institute of Southeast Asian Studies, Singapore. He is also Adjunct Associate Professor at the Southeast Asian Studies Programme, National University of Singapore; Visiting Associate Professor at the Department of Public and Social Administration, City University of Hong Kong; and Editor of the *Penang Economic Monthly*, published by the Socio-Economic and Environmental Research Institute in Penang, Malaysia (www.penangeconomicmonthly.com).

His books include *The Right to Differ: A Biographical Sketch of Lim Kit Siang* (2011); *In Lieu of Ideology: An Intellectual Biography of Goh Keng Swee* (2010); *The Reluctant Politician: Tun Dr Ismail and His Time* (2007); *March 8: Eclipsing May 13* (2008, co-authored with Johan Saravanamuttu and Lee Hock Guan); *Malaya's First Year at the United Nations* (2009, co-compiled with Tawfik Ismail); *Continent, Coast and Ocean: Dynamics of Regionalism in Eastern Asia* (2007, co-edited with Ding Choo Ming); *Lost in Transition: Malaysia under Abdullah* (2008); *Between Umno and a Hard Place: The Najib Razak Era Begins* (2010); *Arrested Reform: The Undoing of Abdullah Badawi* (2009); *The Era of Transition: Malaysia after Mahathir* (2006); and *Chinese Strategists: Beyond Sun Zi's Art of War* (2007).

The Reluctant Politician won the "Award of Excellence for Best Writing Published in Book Form on Any Aspect of Asia (Non-Fiction)" at the Asian Publishing Convention Awards 2008, while *Continent, Coast, Ocean: Dynamics of Regionalism in Eastern Asia* was named "Top Academic Work" in 2008 by the ASEAN Book Publishers Association (ABPA).